Danyeol Moon

English FLY HIGH

✈ Speeding

Global Culture Center

English Fly High
Speeding

Copyright © 2015 by Global Culture Center
All rights reserved.

No part of this publication may be reproduced,
stored in a retrieval system, or transmitted in any form or by any means,
electronic, mechanical, photocopying, recording, or otherwise,
without the prior permission of the publisher.

Global Culture Center
www.the-global.co.kr
Registration No. | 2-407
Registration Date | 15. Dec. 1987
Global Bldg. 4th Floor, 16, Samil-daero 15-gil, Jongno-gu, Seoul, Korea
Tel. 02) 725 – 8282
Fax. 02) 753 – 6969

English Fly High - Speeding
Author | Danyeol Moon
Publisher | Yongboo Kim

Printed in Seoul,
1st Printing - Jan. 2015

ISBN 978-89-8233-255-5 14740
       978-89-8233-250-0 14740 (SET)

About this book

Language learning is like flying an airplane. The first thing that you should do is to be equipped with vocabulary and grammar, with which you assemble the airplane you will eventually fly. The next step is taking off where you will need a huge amount of energy and practical skills along with courage and a certain degree of concentration and commitment. These primary steps not only need to be carried out with patience on the students' side but also be accompanied with well-prepared and carefully designed coursework from the teachers' side. The next step is to fly high with the constant fueling of conversational topics and motivation to the final destination of the proficiency that is required in most standardized spoken tests and interviews of the times. This series of books provides all that is required for the preparation of the flight, guiding the students to acquire the essential volume of vocabulary and expressions and having them internalize the expressions immediately. It also helps students take off into the air, allowing them to actually utilize what they have learned in the previous steps in order for them to get ready for the real-life situations that they will be facing outside of the classes. Finally, this series of books will provide them with the essential topics and high-level skills that are crucial in winning a competitive edge in business as well as in academic pursuits. I hope that everyone who studies with these books will finally reach the destinations that they have been dreaming of.

Danyeol Moon

Contents

Unit	Title	Topic	Function	Grammar
Unit 1 Page 10	Have You Been to Paris?	Personal Experiences	- Describing the Places That You Have Been to - Describing Experiences That You Had There	- Present Perfect Tense: Have/Has + Past Participle
Unit 2 Page 20	How Long Have You Been Doing It?	People's Hobbies and Activities	- Describing the Activities That You Have Been Doing - Describing Things You Like to Do in Your Free Time	- Present Perfect Continuous: Have/Has + Been + Base verb~ing
Unit 3 Page 30	I Should Finish the Project by Today.	Everyday Life at Home and at Work	- Talking about Household Chores - Asking and Answering about *dos* and *don'ts* in Various Situations - Expressing Obligations	- Modals of Obligation: Should + Base verb
Unit 4 Page 40	I Am Taller than My Mother.	Family Members	- Comparing Family Members and Friends - Talking about Personality Traits - Talking about Appearances	- Comparatives: Adjective + -er than ~ - As ~ As
Unit 5 Page 50	Dogs Are the Cutest Animals.	Animals and Pets	- Talking about Pets - Talking about Animals and Zoos	- Superlatives: Adjective + -est

Unit	Title	Topic	Function	Grammar
Unit 6 Page 60	What Do You Plan to Do on the Weekend?	Plans and Appointments	- Talking about Planning for the Future - Arranging and Rearranging of Appointments	- Will / Be Going to / Plan to + Base verb
Unit 7 Page 70	By Whom Was the Speech Delivered?	School [College]	- Talking about School[College] Life - Memories on Younger Years in School	- Passive Voice - Passive with Various Tenses: Passive Negatives, Passive Questions, WH-Questions
Unit 8 Page 80	Flowers Were Given to Me Every Day by You.	Celebrations and Anniversaries	- Talking about Presents - Talking about Activities Celebrating Anniversaries and Holidays	- Passive Voice: Be + P.P. + D.O. / Be + P.P. + to, for, of + I.O.
Unit 9 Page 90	What Is the Price of Your New Smartphone?	Numbers: Under 1,000,000	- Talking with Numbers: Under 1,000,000 - Talking about Prices - Talking about One's Expenses	- Counting Numbers: Under 1,000,000 - To Infinitive (As a Subjective Complement)
Unit 10 Page 100	How Much Does It Cost to Buy a UHD TV?	Numbers: Above 1,000,000	- Talking with Numbers: Above 1,000,000 - Explaining Living Expenses - Talking about Prices of Expensive Things Such as Cars and Houses	- Counting Numbers: Above 1,000,000 - To Infinitive (As a Noun, an Adjective and an Adverb)
Answers	Page 110			
Appendix	Page 122			

Introduction

1. Words & Expressions

Each unit has a list of words that are essential to the composition of the sentences that demonstrate the key objectives and functions of the unit.

2. Grammar

Grammar is crucial even in a conversation book because it is like the iron beams in a building which sustain and stabilize the whole structure. Through abundant examples and exercises, this book makes sure that Korean adult students are able to comprehend the structure of the sentences that they are supposed to speak before they actually start using them.

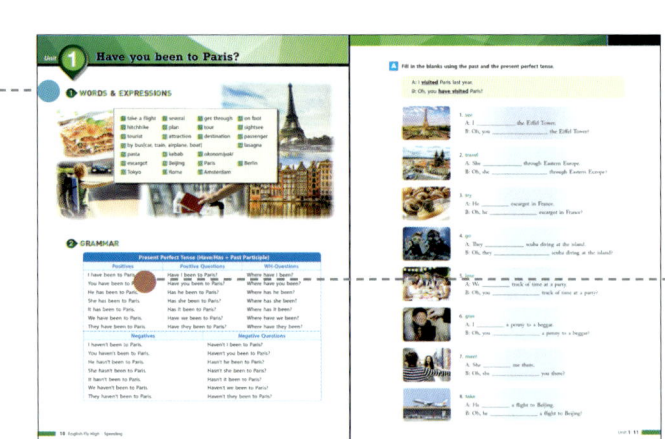

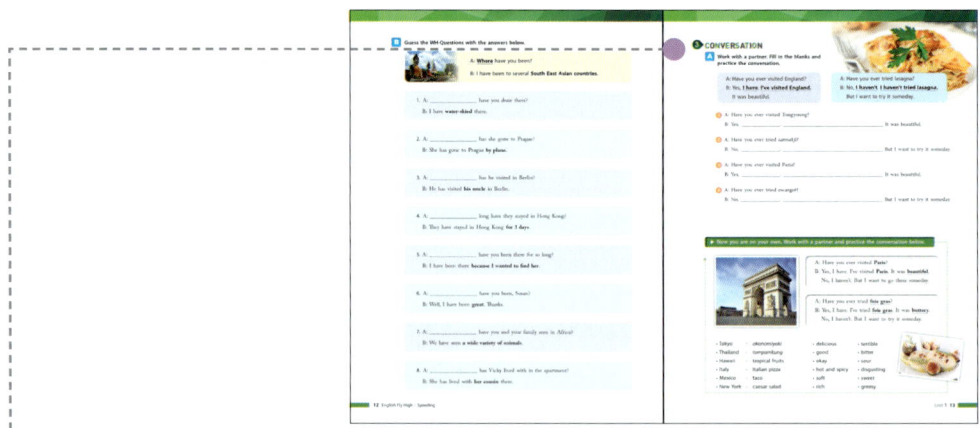

3. Conversation

The conversation exercises have been written based on the principles that the students are fully informed of the context of the interactive language settings and are well-equipped with multiple-intelligence based input as well as opportunities for repetitious practical output performance. Four steps of exercises (A-B-C-D) will help the students gradually and practically build their speaking skills without running out of conversational ideas and expressions. These exercises are easy but they will lead the learners to the objectives of the unit which in most cases means they have fully achieved the comprehension of the grammatical elements and the proficiency in speaking of the target objectives.

4. Reading

Reading must be pleasurable. That means it shouldn't give ESL students a hard time going on and off the text looking up words in the dictionary and wrestling with the meaning of the article. It should be smooth and helping in reinforcing the things that they have newly acquired in the unit. The reading part in this book carries all the features that are portrayed here above. You will enjoy it and you will learn!

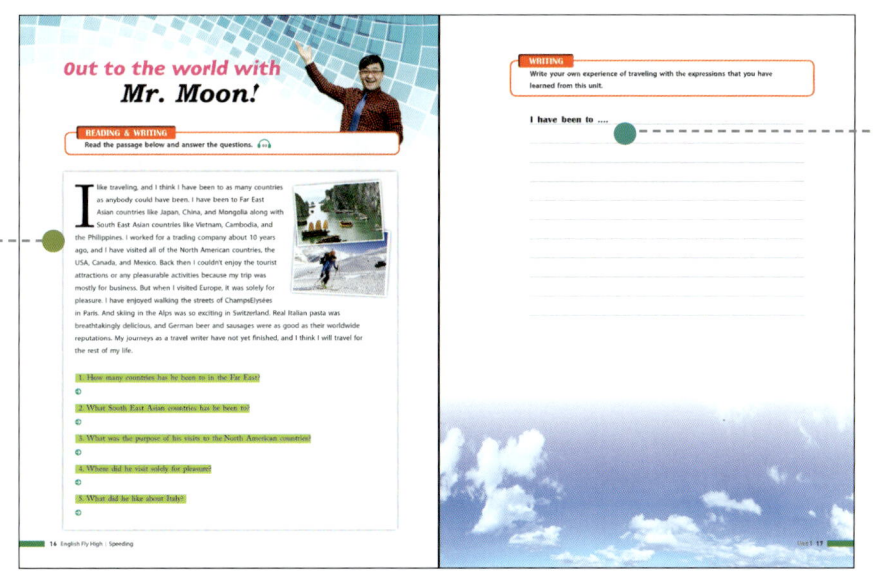

5. Writing

Reception is about mobility whereas production is about fruitfulness. That means that even if you could understand most of the language that is used in this unit, you may not be able to speak or write it on your own, and you could end up not being capable of doing anything "fruitful" for yourself. In most volumes of these books, This "production" part is for speaking.

Introduction 07

Unit 1

Have You Been to Paris?

LESSON PLAN

1 Topic
- Personal Experiences

2 Function
- Describing the Places That You Have Been to
- Describing Experiences That You Had There

3 Grammar
- Present Perfect Tense: Have/Has + Past Participle

1. Have you traveled overseas?
2. Which country have you been to?
3. How did you go there?
4. What tourist attractions have you visited?
5. Have you tried any exotic foods?
6. What have you done at the places?

Unit 1 Have you been to Paris?

1 WORDS & EXPRESSIONS

1. take a flight
2. several
3. get through
4. on foot
5. hitchhike
6. plan
7. tour
8. sightsee
9. tourist
10. attraction
11. destination
12. passenger
13. by bus[car, train, airplane, boat]
14. lasagna
15. pasta
16. kebab
17. okonomiyaki
18. escargot
19. Beijing
20. Paris
21. Berlin
22. Tokyo
23. Rome
24. Amsterdam

2 GRAMMAR

Present Perfect Tense (Have/Has + Past Participle)		
Positives	Positive Questions	WH-Questions
I have been to Paris.	Have I been to Paris?	Where have I been?
You have been to Paris.	Have you been to Paris?	Where have you been?
He has been to Paris.	Has he been to Paris?	Where has he been?
She has been to Paris.	Has she been to Paris?	Where has she been?
It has been to Paris.	Has it been to Paris?	Where has it been?
We have been to Paris.	Have we been to Paris?	Where have we been?
They have been to Paris.	Have they been to Paris?	Where have they been?
Negatives	Negative Questions	
I haven't been to Paris.	Haven't I been to Paris?	
You haven't been to Paris.	Haven't you been to Paris?	
He hasn't been to Paris.	Hasn't he been to Paris?	
She hasn't been to Paris.	Hasn't she been to Paris?	
It hasn't been to Paris.	Hasn't it been to Paris?	
We haven't been to Paris.	Haven't we been to Paris?	
They haven't been to Paris.	Haven't they been to Paris?	

10 English Fly High | Speeding

A Fill in the blanks using the past and the present perfect tense.

> A: I **visited** Paris last year.
> B: Oh, you **have visited** Paris?

1. see
   A: I _____ the Eiffel Tower.
   B: Oh, you _____ the Eiffel Tower?

2. travel
   A: She _____ through Eastern Europe.
   B: Oh, she _____ through Eastern Europe?

3. try
   A: He _____ escargot in France.
   B: Oh, he _____ escargot in France?

4. go
   A: They _____ scuba diving at the island.
   B: Oh, they _____ scuba diving at the island?

5. lose
   A: We _____ track of time at a party.
   B: Oh, you _____ track of time at a party?

6. give
   A: I _____ a penny to a beggar.
   B: Oh, you _____ a penny to a beggar?

7. meet
   A: She _____ me there.
   B: Oh, she _____ you there?

8. take
   A: He _____ a flight to Beijing.
   B: Oh, he _____ a flight to Beijing?

Unit 1 11

B Guess the WH-Questions with the answers below.

A: **Where** have you been?

B: I have been to several **South East Asian countries**.

1. A: _____ have you done there?
   B: I have **water-skied** there.

2. A: _____ has she gone to Prague?
   B: She has gone to Prague **by plane**.

3. A: _____ has he visited in Berlin?
   B: He has visited **his uncle** in Berlin.

4. A: _____ long have they stayed in Hong Kong?
   B: They have stayed in Hong Kong **for 3 days**.

5. A: _____ have you been there for so long?
   B: I have been there **because I wanted to find her**.

6. A: _____ have you been, Susan?
   B: Well, I have been **great**. Thanks.

7. A: _____ have you and your family seen in Africa?
   B: We have seen **a wide variety of animals**.

8. A: _____ has Vicky lived with in the apartment?
   B: She has lived with **her cousin** there.

3 CONVERSATION

A Work with a partner. Fill in the blanks and practice the conversation.

A: Have you ever visited England?
B: Yes, **I have**. **I've visited England.** It was beautiful.

A: Have you ever tried lasagna?
B: No, **I haven't**. **I haven't tried lasagna.** But I want to try it someday.

① A: Have you ever visited Tongyoung?
   B: Yes, _____. _____ It was beautiful.

② A: Have you ever tried *sannakji*?
   B: No, _____. _____ But I want to try it someday.

③ A: Have you ever visited Paris?
   B: Yes, _____. _____ It was beautiful.

④ A: Have you ever tried escargot?
   B: No, _____. _____ But I want to try it someday.

▶ Now you are on your own. Work with a partner and practice the conversation below.

A: Have you ever visited **Paris**?
B: Yes, I have. I've visited **Paris**. It was **beautiful**. /
   No, I haven't. But I want to go there someday.

A: Have you ever tried **foie gras**?
B: Yes, I have. I've tried **foie gras**. It was **buttery**. /
   No, I haven't. But I want to try it someday.

- Tokyo   - okonomiyaki
- Thailand   - tomyamkung
- Hawaii   - tropical fruits
- Italy   - Italian pizza
- Mexico   - taco
- New York   - caesar salad

- delicious
- good
- okay
- hot and spicy
- soft
- rich

- terrible
- bitter
- sour
- disgusting
- sweet
- greasy

Unit **1** 13

B Work with a partner. Fill in the blanks and practice the conversation.

A: Where have you been for your last vacation?
B: **I've been to Rome.**

A: What have you done there?
B: **I've visited the Colosseum.**

1. **Los Angeles / visit Universal Studios**

   A: Where have you been for your last vacation?
   B: _____
   A: What have you done there?
   B: _____

2. **Beijing / see the Forbidden City**

   A: Where have you been for your last vacation?
   B: _____
   A: What have you done there?
   B: _____

3. **Busan / eat raw fish**

   A: Where have you been for your last vacation?
   B: _____
   A: What have you done there?
   B: _____

4. **Egypt / learn belly dancing**

   A: Where have you been for your last vacation?
   B: _____
   A: What have you done there?
   B: _____

▶ Now you are on your own.

A: Where have you been for your winter[summer, last] vacation?
B: **I've been to Washington D.C.**
A: What have you done there?
B: **I've visited the White House.**

- Mongolia / ride horses
- Thailand / swim in the ocean
- Tsingdao / drink Tsingdao beer
- Damyang / try *tukgalbi*
- Yeosu / vist the Expo
- Kwangju / climb Mudeung mountain

C Work with a partner. Fill in the blanks and practice the conversation. 🎧02

> A: **I've traveled to northern China** this vacation.
> B: You have? How did you get there?
> A: I went there **by plane**. It took about **4 hours**.

1. **be to Amsterdam / by plane / 10 hours**

   A: _____ this vacation.

   B: You have? How did you get there?

   A: I went there _____. It took about _____.

2. **visit Denver / by train / 14 hours**

   A: _____ this vacation.

   B: You have? How did you get there?

   A: I went there _____. It took about _____.

3. **be to Toronto / by bus / 5 hours**

   A: _____ this vacation.

   B: You have? How did you get there?

   A: I went there _____. It took about _____.

4. **travel through the Amazon / on foot / 14 days**

   A: _____ this vacation.

   B: You have? How did you get through?

   A: I got through _____. It took about _____.

▶ Work with a partner. Suppose you are a famous travel writer and you have been to many countries and have experienced many things. You are now visiting a school to give a lecture to curious students. Your partner is one of them and he or she is asking you the questions below. Try to answer to the questions on your own.

1. Have you traveled to any overseas[domestic] countries[areas]?
   ex. Yes, I have. I have been to Turkey.

2. Which country[Which part of the country] have you been to?
   ex. I have been to Turkey and visited Istanbul, the capital city of Turkey.

3. How did you go[get] there?
   ex. I went[got] there by airplane. It took about 10 hours.

4. What tourist attractions have you visited?
   ex. I have visited the St. Sophia Cathedral in Istanbul. It was beautiful.

Out to the world with Mr. Moon!

READING & WRITING
Read the passage below and answer the questions.

I like traveling, and I think I have been to as many countries as anybody could have been. I have been to Far East Asian countries like Japan, China, and Mongolia along with South East Asian countries like Vietnam, Cambodia, and the Philippines. I worked for a trading company about 10 years ago, and I have visited all of the North American countries, the USA, Canada, and Mexico. Back then I couldn't enjoy the tourist attractions or any pleasurable activities because my trip was mostly for business. But when I visited Europe, it was solely for pleasure. I have enjoyed walking the streets of ChampsElysées in Paris. And skiing in the Alps was so exciting in Switzerland. Real Italian pasta was breathtakingly delicious, and German beer and sausages were as good as their worldwide reputations. My journeys as a travel writer have not yet finished, and I think I will travel for the rest of my life.

1. How many countries has he been to in the Far East?
→

2. What South East Asian countries has he been to?
→

3. What was the purpose of his visits to the North American countries?
→

4. Where did he visit solely for pleasure?
→

5. What did he like about Italy?
→

WRITING

Write your own experience of traveling with the expressions that you have learned from this unit.

I have been to ....

Unit 1 17

Unit 2

How Long Have You Been Doing It?

LESSON PLAN

① Topic
- People's Hobbies and Activities

② Function
- Describing the Activities That You Have Been Doing
- Describing Things You Like to Do in Your Free Time

③ Grammar
- Present Perfect Continuous: Have/Has + Been + Base verb~ing

1. What kinds of hobbies[activities] do you practice?
2. When did you start doing them?
3. How long have you been doing them?
4. Have you ever stopped doing them?
5. What made you quit the activities?
6. Do you plan to take up any other activities?

Unit 2 How long have you been doing it?

1 WORDS & EXPRESSIONS

1. play the drums
2. culinary arts
3. practice dance sports
4. blog
5. knit
6. yacht
7. practice Pilates
8. ride a motor bike
9. ride a mountain bike
10. go rafting
11. go snowboarding
12. play chess
13. make jewelry
14. compose music
15. write songs
16. collect stamps
17. collect coins
18. collect antiques
19. make wine
20. speed skate
21. go hiking
22. quit
23. nook and cranny
24. learn sign languages
25. get tired of
26. deal with
27. keep off
28. take up
29. graduate from

2 GRAMMAR

Present Perfect Continuous (Have/Has + Been + Base verb~ing)	
Positives	Positive Questions
I have been doing it.	Have I been doing it?
You have been doing it.	Have you been doing it?
He has been doing it.	Has he been doing it?
She has been doing it.	Has she been doing it?
We have been doing it.	Have we been doing it?
They have been doing it.	Have they been doing it?
Negatives	Negative Questions
I haven't been doing it.	Haven't I been doing it?
You haven't been doing it.	Haven't you been doing it?
He hasn't been doing it.	Hasn't he been doing it?
She hasn't been doing it.	Hasn't she been doing it?
We haven't been doing it.	Haven't we been doing it?
They haven't been doing it.	Haven't they been doing it?

A Fill in the blanks using the present perfect continuous.

> A: Wow, you are so good at dancing!
> B: Thanks. Actually, I **have been going** to a dance academy for a long time.

1. **learn**
   A: Your food is lovely.
   B: Thanks. Actually, I _____ how to cook for a long time.

2. **play**
   A: Your sister is a wonderful pianist.
   B: Thanks. Actually, she _____ the piano since she was a little girl.

3. **drive**
   A: Adam knows every nook and cranny of this town!
   B: Come on! He _____ in this city all his life.

4. **sing**
   A: Wow, her voice is heavenly.
   B: That's right. She _____ in front of audiences for years.

5. **practice**
   A: You knocked down all the bad guys.
   B: Well, I _____ *Taekwondo* since I was 10 years old.

6. **attend**
   A: Thank you for the nice dinner. All the food was terrific.
   B: Thanks. Actually, I _____ a culinary arts institute since last January.

7. **race**
   A: Watch out! You are going to bump into the wall.
   B: Don't worry. I _____ all my life.

B Fill in the blanks with either *for* or *since*.

A: I have been practicing dance sports ever **since** I was 5 years old.

B: Wow, it means that you have been dancing **for** 20 years!

1. A: He has been seeing me _____ 2011.

   B: You have been dating him _____ 4 years!

2. A: She has been composing _____ she met you.

   B: You mean she has been writing songs _____ 3 years?

3. A: Have you been losing weight _____ the beginning of the month?

   B: Yes, I have. I have been working out at the gym _____ weeks.

4. A: We have been keeping off fatty foods _____ 8 weeks.

   B: So, you have been staying away from fatty foods _____ I last saw you guys?

5. A: They have been eating out on Saturday evenings _____ the end of last year.

   B: Really? They have been dining in a restaurant on Saturday evenings _____ a year?

6. A: I have been dealing with this matter _____ last week.

   B: Oh, dear, you have been dealing with it _____ a week and a half?

7. A: Hey, I haven't seen you _____ so long.

   B: Right. We haven't seen each other _____ almost a year.

3 CONVERSATION

A Work with a partner. Fill in the blanks and practice the conversation.

> A: How long **have** you **been practicing yoga**?
> B: I started it in **2010**, and **I have been practicing it** ever since.

① study Chinese / last year

A: How long _____ your brother _____?

B: He started it _____, and _____ ever since.

② learn sign languages / 10 years ago

A: How long _____ you _____?

B: I started it _____, and _____ ever since.

③ play the drums / in high school

A: How long _____ Helen _____?

B: She started it _____, and _____ ever since.

④ make wine / when he was 20 years old

A: How long _____ his father _____?

B: He started it _____, and _____ ever since.

▶ Now you are on your own. Use the words in the box. Fill in the blanks and practice with your classmates about what you have been doing.

A: What do you do for a hobby?
B: My hobby is to **go bowling**.
A: How long **have you been going bowling**?
B: I have been doing it for a year. / I have been doing it since last year.

Hobbies and Activities	go bowling, go rafting, go camping, go hiking, go snowboarding, play chess, play golf, play the piano, play the guitar, play the drums
Duration	for 4 days, for 5 years, for a life time, for ages, for 3 months, for at least a few months, all my life
The Time You Started	when I was born, when I was a kid, when I graduated from college, when I was at middle school, when I first met you

B Work with a partner. Fill in the blanks and practice the conversation.

A: What do you do for a hobby?
B: I took up **playing golf** 3 years ago and **have been playing golf** ever since.

A: What else are you interested in?
B: I **have gone scuba diving** once, but I quit.

1. **cook Chinese foods / cook Japanese foods**

   A: What does your wife do for a hobby?
   B: She took up _____ 3 years ago and _____ ever since.
   A: What else is she interested in?
   B: She _____ once, but she quit.

2. **ride a mountain bike / ride a motor bike**

   A: What do you do for a hobby?
   B: I took up _____ 3 years ago and _____ ever since.
   A: What else are you interested in?
   B: I _____ once, but I quit.

3. **belly dance / collect antiques**

   A: What does Stella do for a hobby?
   B: She took up _____ 3 years ago and _____ ever since.
   A: What else is she interested in?
   B: She _____ once, but she quit.

▶ Now you are on your own. Use the words in the box. Fill in the blanks and practice with your classmates about what you have been doing and what you had done before.

A: What do you do for a hobby?
B: I started to **play golf** 3 years ago and have been playing golf ever since.
A: **Have you been playing golf** today?
B: No, **I have been swimming** today.

Hobbies and Activities

- blog
- travel
- cycle
- collect antiques
- make jewelry
- write songs
- compose music
- practice Pilates
- collect stamps
- go-kart race
- play video games

C Work with a partner. Fill in the blanks and practice the conversation. 🎧 05

> A: I quit **boxing**.
> B: What made you do that?
> A: I quit it because **I got hurt all the time**.
> B: Oh, that's too bad.

1. **yacht / it cost too much money**

    A: I quit _____.

    B: What made you do that?

    A: I quit it because _____.

    B: Oh, that's too bad.

2. **knit / my eyes were sore**

    A: I quit _____.

    B: What made you do that?

    A: I quit it because _____.

    B: Oh, that's too bad.

3. **speed skate / it was too cold**

    A: I quit _____.

    B: What made you do that?

    A: I quit it because _____.

    B: Oh, that's too bad.

▶ Work with a partner. Suppose you are a market researcher and you are looking into people's hobbies through the phone. You are asking these questions.

1. Do you practice any hobbies?
   ex. Yes, I do. Actually, I go swimming every day.

2. How long have you been doing it?
   ex. I have been swimming for 3 months, and I like it so much better than my last hobby.

3. What was your previous hobby?
   ex. I had played golf for 4 years.

4. Why did you quit it?
   ex. I quit golfing because it took too much time.

5. Do you want to take up any other activities in the future?
   ex. I want to take up kung fu someday because I want to protect myself.

Out to the world with Mr. Moon!

READING & WRITING
Read the passage below and answer the questions.

Tommy is a hobby-seeker. Now he enjoys skydiving and has been doing it for 2 months, but he went scuba diving just before that. Actually he is a very fast learner. When he started chess, even before he took up scuba diving, he won the community chess championship only after he had learned it for 3 weeks. He constantly changes his hobbies. One reason is that he picks up things so fast but another reason is that he gets tired of things so fast, too. Last year when he took up *karate*, it took less than a month before he quit it because he got sick of the form practice. When he started coin collecting, he spent all his savings and collected every coin in the town. But there is one thing that he has been doing all his life ever since he was a little boy. That is hobby-seeking itself. That's right. He will remain seeking hobbies all his life.

1. What was the activity Tommy did before he started skydiving?
→

2. Was he good at the form practice of *karate*?
→

3. For how long did he learn chess before he won the community chess championship?
→

4. What activity made him use up all his savings?
→

5. What is the one thing that he has been doing all his life?
→

WRITING

Write your own experience of your free time activities and hobbies with the expressions that you have learned from this unit.

I took up playing golf 3 years ago and have been playing golf ever since.

Unit 3

I Should Finish the Project by Today.

LESSON PLAN

1 Topic
- Everyday Life at Home and at Work

2 Function
- Talking about Household Chores
- Asking and Answering about *dos* and *don'ts* in Various Situations
- Expressing Obligations

3 Grammar
- Modals of Obligation: Should + Base verb

1. What kinds of household chores should you do every day?
2. What do you have to do on weekdays?
3. What do you do (for a living)?
4. What are some *dos* for your job?
5. What are some *don'ts* for your job?
6. What do you think parents should do for their children?

Unit 3 I should finish the project by today.

1 WORDS & EXPRESSIONS

1. support one's family
2. pay house loans off
3. obey one's parents
4. household chores
5. put on gloves
6. take off shoes
7. take out the garbage
8. send a parcel
9. apologize in public
10. break an appointment
11. sponsor a charity organization
12. get the credit for graduation
13. supervisor
14. supervise
15. make typos
16. get a raise
17. seek a job
18. colleague
19. clerk
20. part-timer
21. employee
22. boss
23. subordinate

2 GRAMMAR

| Modals of Obligation (Should + Base verb) ||
Positives	Questions
I should do it.	Should I do it?
You should do it.	Should you do it?
He should do it.	Should he do it?
She should do it.	Should she do it?
We should do it.	Should we do it?
They should do it.	Should they do it?
Negatives	Negative Questions
I shouldn't do it.	Shouldn't I do it?
You shouldn't do it.	Shouldn't you do it?
He shouldn't do it.	Shouldn't he do it?
She shouldn't do it.	Shouldn't she do it?
We shouldn't do it.	Shouldn't we do it?
They shouldn't do it.	Shouldn't they do it?

• More modals of obligation: must, have to, ought to, be supposed to, be obliged to, need to

A Choose the correct modal.

A: I am supposed to take care of my little brother.
B: You mean you (**should** / may) babysit him?

1. A: He is obliged to finish the project.
   B: You mean he (can / must) finish the project?

2. A: My sister works for money.
   B: You mean she (has to / likes to) work?

3. A: I bring home the bacon.
   B: You mean you (love to / ought to) support your family?

4. A: It's freezing outside. You'd better put on your gloves when you go out.
   B: You mean I (could / need to) put them on?

5. A: She has a big mouth. So you have to watch your tongue.
   B: You mean I (should / would) hold my tongue in front of her?

6. A: I don't think Anne can take care of everything by herself.
   B: You mean she (ought to / want to) get help from someone?

7. A: The meeting will be held at 10 o'clock tomorrow morning.
   B: You mean I will (be able to / have to) finish the report today?

8. A: Father will come back from his business trip today.
   B: You mean we (must / can) get home early this evening?

Unit 3 31

B Look at the model conversations and fill in the blanks.

> A: Should he **take out the garbage** every day?
> B: Yes, **he should**. He should take out the **garbage** every day.

> A: Do I have to go to school on Sunday?
> B: No, **you don't**. You don't have to go **to school** on Sunday.

1. go on a strike

   A: Should we _____ from now on?

   B: Yes, _____. _____ from now on.

2. get the credit for graduation

   A: Does Marian have to _____?

   B: No, _____. _____

3. work out for your health

   A: Should you _____ every day?

   B: Yes, _____. _____ every day.

4. take off our shoes

   A: Do we have to _____ here?

   B: No, _____. _____ here.

5. eat only fruits and vegetables

   A: Should I _____?

   B: Yes, _____. _____

6. help their son with his homework

   A: Do the Johnsons have to _____?

   B: No, _____. _____

7. apologize in public

   A: Should the president(he) _____?

   B: Yes, _____. _____

8. go out

   A: Do you have to _____ right now?

   B: No, _____. _____ right now.

3 CONVERSATION

A Work with a partner. Fill in the blanks and practice the conversation.

A: Should I clean the room every morning?
B: Yes, **you should clean the room** every morning.

A: Should I work every day?
B: No, **you don't have to work** every day.

1. A: Should Bill attend the class all through the semester?
   B: Yes, _____ all through the semester.

2. A: Should she supervise the part-timers every single day?
   B: No, _____ every single day.

3. A: Should the employees get a raise next year?
   B: Yes, _____ next year.

4. A: Should I send a parcel to Betty right away?
   B: No, _____ right away.

▶ Now you are on your own. Use the words in the box. Fill in the blanks and practice with your classmates about your duties.

A: What should you do every morning?
B: I should **feed the dog** and **make breakfast** every morning.
A: Should you **prepare your lunch**, too?
B: No, I don't have to.

Household Chores

• make the bed	• make dinner	• set the table	• wash the dishes
• do the laundry	• iron clothes	• do the vacuuming	• sweep the floor
• clean the room	• do the shopping	• feed the pet	• mow the lawn
• water the plants	• take out the garbage		

Unit 3 33

B Work with a partner. Fill in the blanks and practice the conversation.

A: Why do you work so hard?
B: Because I have to **support my family**.

A: You must **pay for your kid's college education**, too?
B: I don't have to, but I want to.

1. **finish this project by 5 o'clock / do your chemistry homework**

   A: Why do you work so hard?
   B: Because I have to _____.
   A: You must _____, too?
   B: I don't have to, but I want to.

2. **give my kid some allowance / give your mom some allowance**

   A: Why do you work so hard?
   B: Because I have to _____.
   A: You must _____, too?
   B: I don't have to, but I want to.

3. **pay house loans off / sponsor a charity organization**

   A: Why do you work so hard?
   B: Because I have to _____.
   A: You must _____, too?
   B: I don't have to, but I want to.

▶ Now you are on your own. Use the words in the box. Fill in the blanks and practice with your classmates about what you ought to do as a parent or a kid.

A: What should you do **as a father**?
B: I should **support my family**.
A: You must **do household chores**, too?
B: I don't have to, but I want to.

Roles: a father, a mother, a son, a daughter, a boss, a supervisor, a subordinate, a part-timer, a teacher

Jobs: support one's family, do household chores, obey one's parents, study hard, watch how they work, help my boss, clean the store, help run the store

C Work with a partner. Fill in the blanks and practice the conversation. 🎧 08

> A: Tell me about the *dos* and *don'ts* as a business man.
> B: Well, you should **always be on time**.
> A: What about *don'ts*?
> B: Hmm. You shouldn't **break appointments on short notice**.

1. **work with style / get fat**

   A: Tell me about the *dos* and *don'ts* as a model.

   B: Well, you should _____.

   A: What about *don'ts*?

   B: Hmm. You shouldn't _____.

2. **be very meticulous / make typos**

   A: Tell me about the *dos* and *don'ts* as a clerk.

   B: Well, you should _____.

   A: What about *don'ts*?

   B: Hmm. You shouldn't _____.

▶ Work with a partner. Suppose you are seeking a job and you are asking advice of somebody about a successful job interview. Ask and answer the questions about the *dos* and *don'ts* of job interviews like below.

> A: What are the things that I should do for an interview?
> B: Well, you have to **arrive 10 minutes early**.
> A: What are the things that I shouldn't do for an interview?
> B: Hmm. You're not supposed to **be late**.

Dos	Don'ts
• prepare and practice for the interview	• just memorize your answers
• check the location where you're having the interview	• chew gum during the interview
• shake hands firmly	• have a limp handshake
• make eye contact with your interviewer	• use poor language and slang
• show enthusiasm for the position	• be overly aggressive
• answer questions truthfully and frankly	• say anything negative about former colleagues or supervisors

Unit 3 35

Out to the world with Mr. Moon!

READING & WRITING
Read the passage below and answer the questions.

Mr. Kim is a middle aged man. His life is full of obligations. He should get up early to get ready for work. He has to work out every day to stay healthy. He thinks his health is not only his but also his family's. He has to do his best to make the most out of his resources and make the most money in his job. He must keep good relationships with his business partners and his boss or he should suffer less income due to a poor outcome at work. He must be punctual and precise in completing the missions that he has been assigned to. When he returns home, he must be a caring and loving father to his teenage daughter as well as a loving husband to his beloved wife. Mr. Kim's life is full of duties, but he fulfills them all with a sense of responsibility that comes solely from love.

1. What is a middle aged man's life like?
➡

2. What does he think about his health?
➡

3. What will happen if he doesn't keep good relationships with his business partners?
➡

4. Who does he have to be to his daughter at home?
➡

5. With what does he fulfill all his duties?
➡

WRITING

Write your own *dos* and *don'ts* at home(as a father, mother, daughter, son) or at work(as a boss, supervisor, subordinate, colleague).

Dos

I should obey my parents as a daughter.

Don'ts

I shouldn't tell a lie to my family.

Unit 4

I Am Taller than My Mother.

LESSON PLAN

❶ Topic
- Family Members

❷ Function
- Comparing Family Members and Friends
- Talking about Personality Traits
- Talking about Appearances

❸ Grammar
- Comparatives: Adjective + -er than ~
- As ~ As

1. How do your family members look? Can you compare them?
2. What do your close friends look like? Can you compare them?
3. Can you tell me about the personality traits of your family members in comparison?
4. Can you tell me about the personality traits of your close friends in comparison?
5. Tell me who your favorite star is and compare him or her with an average person.
6. Tell me about someone you admire and compare him or her with yourself.

Unit 4 I am taller than my mother.

1 WORDS & EXPRESSIONS

1 popular	2 fancy	3 understanding
4 intriguing	5 thrilling	6 meaningful
7 touching	8 twisted	9 provoking
10 scary	11 boring	12 breathtaking
13 spectacular	14 hilarious	15 disgusting
16 unique	17 meticulous	18 caring
19 tolerant	20 organized	21 take after
22 cold / warm	23 tough / soft	24 strong / weak
25 thin / heavy, fat	26 expensive / cheap	27 tall / short
28 pretty, beautiful / ugly	29 slim, slender / chubby	30 charming / unattractive

31 fair-skinned / dark-skinned
32 good-looking / bad looking, homely looking

2 GRAMMAR

Comparatives (Adjective + -er than ~)	
Positives	**Positive Questions**
I'm taller than John.	Am I taller than John?
You're taller than John.	Are you taller than John?
He's taller than John.	Is he taller than John?
She's taller than John.	Is she taller than John?
It's taller than John.	Is it taller than John?
We're taller than John.	Are we taller than John?
They're taller than John.	Are they taller than John?
Negatives	**Negative Questions**
I'm not taller than John.	Aren't I taller than John?
You're not taller than John.	Aren't you taller than John?
He's not taller than John.	Isn't he taller than John?
She's not taller than John.	Isn't she taller than John?
It's not taller than John.	Isn't it taller than John?
We're not taller than John.	Aren't we taller than John?
They're not taller than John.	Aren't they taller than John?

- tall → taller
- easy → easier (y → i)
- big → bigger
- good → better
- beautiful → more beautiful
- bad → worse

A Fill in the blanks with a comparative.

A: I am short, but he is tall.
B: Oh, he is **taller** than you!

1. **thin**
   A: She is thin, but he is fat.
   B: Oh, she is _____ than he!

2. **rich**
   A: They are poor, but we are rich.
   B: Oh, we are _____ than they!

3. **beautiful**
   A: Jane is beautiful, but her sister is not.
   B: Oh, Jane is _____ than her sister!

4. **strong**
   A: His sister was weak before, but she is strong now.
   B: His sister is _____ than before!

5. **delicious**
   A: The pie is delicious, but the sandwich doesn't taste good.
   B: The pie is _____ than the sandwich!

6. **heavy**
   A: Karen's rabbit is heavy, but my dog is light.
   B: Karen's rabbit is _____ than my dog!

7. **expensive**
   A: These shoes are expensive, but those shoes are cheap.
   B: These shoes are _____ than those shoes!

B Fill in the blanks with either *as ~ as* or *not as ~ as*.

A: Tom is 6 feet tall, and John is also 6 feet tall.
B: John is **as tall as** Tom.

A: Julie weighs 150 pounds, but Lucy weighs 120 pounds.
B: Lucy is **not as heavy as** Julie.

1. **smart**
   A: Tim scored 800 on the test, and Josh also scored the same.
   B: Josh is _____ Tim.

2. **funny**
   A: Jay likes to joke all day long, but Harry rarely tells jokes.
   B: Harry is _____ Jay.

3. **old**
   A: My grandmother is 75 years old, and Mrs. Smith is of the same age.
   B: Mrs. Smith is _____ my grandmother.

4. **popular**
   A: Everybody admires James, but few people like Mat.
   B: Mat is _____ James.

5. **late**
   A: Both Tim and Cathy arrived at the office at 10 o'clock this morning.
   B: Cathy was _____ Tim this morning.

6. **crowded**
   A: There are a lot of people on this street, but there are few people on that street.
   B: That street is _____ this street.

7. **friendly**
   A: My dog really likes people, and Kimberly's cat likes people, too.
   B: Kimberly's cat is _____ my dog.

3 CONVERSATION

A Work with a partner. Fill in the blanks and practice the conversation.

> A: Is your brother tall?
> B: He is **taller than me but shorter than my dad**.

1 tough, Mr. Smith / soft, Mr. Sosa

A: Is your teacher tough?

B: He is _____.

2 slim, Jane / chubby, June

A: Is Nancy slim?

B: She is _____.

3 cold, yesterday / warm, last Sunday

A: Is it cold today?

B: It is _____.

4 expensive, yours / cheap, Paula's

A: Is your cell phone expensive?

B: It is _____.

▶ Now you are on your own.
Student A: Ask questions about the looks of your partner's family.
Student B: Answer questions comparing your family members as the example.

A: How does your mom look?
B: **She is very tall**.
A: **Is she taller** than you?
B: Yes, **she is taller** than me, but **shorter than my dad**.

Appearance

- tall / short
- slim, slender / chubby
- thin / heavy, fat
- strong / weak
- fair-skinned / dark-skinned
- charming / unattractive
- pretty, beautiful / ugly
- good-looking / bad looking, homely looking

B Work with a partner. Fill in the blanks and practice the conversation.

A: How **tall** is your brother?
B: He is **as tall as I am(=me)**.

A: **Is he as tall as your dad**?
B: No, he is not **as tall as my dad(=him)**.

1. **smart / Mr. Moon / Einstein**

   A: How _____ is your sister?
   B: She is _____.
   A: Is she _____?
   B: No, she is not _____.

2. **big / a calf / a cow**

   A: How _____ is your dog?
   B: It is _____.
   A: Is it _____?
   B: No, it is not _____.

3. **handsome / his brother / Tom Cruise**

   A: How _____ is your husband?
   B: He is _____.
   A: Is he _____?
   B: No, he is not _____.

▶ Now you are on your own. Compare the stuff or people around you using *as ~ as*.

A: How **beautiful** is your **girlfriend**?
B: **She** is **as beautiful as Emma Watson**. /
   She is not **as beautiful as Emma Watson**.

- fancy / car / a BMW
- big / house / a castle
- old / dad / my dad
- sweet / boyfriend / honey
- good / eye sight / hawk

- fluent / English / a native American
- cute / daughter / a puppy
- comfortable / bed / sleeping on a cloud
- thin / son / a piece of paper
- young / grandma / your mom

C Work with a partner. Fill in the blanks and practice the conversation. 🎧

> **bad / problem**
>
> A: How **bad** is your **problem**?
> B: It is **much worse** than I thought.
> A: Really? What makes you say that?

① understanding / your new boss

A: How _____ is _____?

B: He is _____ than I thought.

A: Really? What makes you say that?

② intriguing / Christopher Nolan's new movie

A: How _____ is _____?

B: It is _____ than I thought.

A: Really? What makes you say that?

③ late / the announcement

A: How _____ is _____?

B: It is _____ _____ than I thought.

A: Really? What makes you say that?

▶ Work with a partner. Think of the movies that you have seen so far and compare them with your partner. Refer to the model conversation below in case.

> A: How did you like the movie *Interstellar*?
> B: It was **okay**, but not as **fun** as the movie *Gravity*.
> A: What makes you say that?
> B: Well, *Gravity* is much **more dramatic** than *Interstellar*.

• fun	• funny	• thrilling	• meaningful	• sad
• moving	• touching	• twisted	• long	• provoking
• terrible	• scary	• boring	• breathtaking	• fantastic
• spectacular	• hilarious	• disgusting		

Unit 4 45

Out to the world with Mr. Moon!

READING & WRITING
Read the passage below and answer the questions.

Joseph has a family of four. Everybody in his family is very unique. His father is short and fat. He is more meticulous than anyone in his family, but not as understanding as his mother. His mother isn't as caring as his father, but she is much more tolerant than him. She considers herself a bohemian. She travels through countries even when her kids are in school, but Joseph and his sister don't care about it at all. Joseph, in fact, is a very smart student, but he is not nearly as smart as his sister, Jane. Jane is far more organized than Joseph. It seems like she takes after her father. But she is much taller than her father. Actually she is as tall as her mother. Joseph looks much like his father. He is just as short and fat as his father.

1. Who is more meticulous than others?
→

2. Who is more understanding between his father and his mother?
→

3. Who takes after the father in character?
→

4. Is Joseph's father taller than his mother?
→

5. Who is as tall as Joseph?
→

WRITING

Write your own story about your family. Talk about appearances of your family members and compare them with the expressions that you have learned from this unit.

I have a family of five.

My Dad is huge and strong, about 6.2 feet tall.

Unit 5

Dogs Are the Cutest Animals.

LESSON PLAN

1 Topic
- Animals and Pets

2 Function
- Talking about Pets
- Talking about Animals and Zoos

3 Grammar
- Superlatives: Adjective + -est

1. Do you have a pet?
2. Why do you like[dislike] pets?
3. Do you like to go to the zoo?
4. What kinds of animals do you like the most?
5. What are the most beautiful pets or animals on the earth?
6. What are the most unique animals on the earth?

Unit 5 Dogs are the cutest animals.

1 WORDS & EXPRESSIONS

1. cicada
2. puppy
3. kitten
4. lizard
5. tropical fish
6. species
7. panda
8. sloth
9. grizzly bear
10. hyena
11. peacock
12. jelly fish
13. rhinoceros
14. beagle
15. spaniel
16. porcupine
17. parrot
18. canary
19. giraffe
20. iguana
21. ferret
22. snail
23. turtle
24. seal
25. prairie dog
26. leopard
27. dolphin
28. koala
29. alligator
30. cockroach
31. black mamba
32. creepy
33. tiny
34. tidy
35. adorable
36. lazy
37. poisonous
38. fierce
39. splendid
40. rare
41. hyperactive
42. messy
43. filthy
44. extinct
45. environment
46. planet
47. calculate

2 GRAMMAR

| Superlatives (Adjective + -est) ||
Positives	Positive Questions
I'm the tallest.	Am I the tallest?
You're the tallest.	Are you the tallest?
He's the tallest.	Is he the tallest?
She's the tallest.	Is she the tallest?
It's the tallest.	Is it the tallest?
We're the tallest.	Are we the tallest?
They're the tallest.	Are they the tallest?
Negatives	Negative Questions
I'm not the tallest.	Aren't I the tallest?
You're not the tallest.	Aren't you the tallest?
He's not the tallest.	Isn't he the tallest?
She's not the tallest.	Isn't she the tallest?
It's not the tallest.	Isn't it the tallest?
We're not the tallest.	Aren't we the tallest?
They're not the tallest.	Aren't they the tallest?

- big → the biggest
- funny → the funniest (y → i)
- beautiful → the most beautiful

A Fill in the blanks with a superlative.

> A: This puppy is very cute.
> B: I think it's **the cutest** puppy in this pet shop.

1. **wild**
   A: It looks like the alligator is very wild.
   B: I think the alligator is _____ animal of all.

2. **expensive**
   A: I hear that Siberian tigers are very expensive.
   B: I think they are _____ animals in the world.

3. **lazy**
   A: They say that koalas are extremely lazy.
   B: I think they are _____ animals on the planet.

4. **friendly**
   A: Everyone says my cat is as friendly as a dog.
   B: I think my cat is _____ cat in my neighborhood.

5. **tiny**
   A: This lizard is so tiny I can hardly find it.
   B: I think it's _____ lizard in the world.

6. **quiet**
   A: Tropical fish are very quiet pets, I know.
   B: I think fish are _____ pets of all.

7. **unbelievable**
   A: Don't you think a chameleon is an unbelievable creature?
   B: I think it's _____ creature in the world.

B Fill in the blanks with a comparative.

> A: What do you think of Kim, Yuna?
> B: I think she **skates more beautifully than any other skater** in the world.

> A: What do you think of Park, Taehwan?
> B: I think he **swims faster than any other swimmer** in Asia.

1. **smile brightly / gymnast**
   A: What do you think of Soen, Yunjae?
   B: I think she _____ in the world.

2. **dress well / boy**
   A: What do you think of Daniel?
   B: I think he _____ in the class.

3. **try hard / player**
   A: What do you think of Ryu, Hyunjin?
   B: I think he _____ in America.

4. **calculate quickly / student**
   A: What do you think of Julia?
   B: I think she _____ in my school.

5. **draw creatively / painter**
   A: What do you think of Picasso?
   B: I think he _____ in the world.

6. **act naturally / actor**
   A: What do you think of Song, Gangho?
   B: I think he _____ in Korea.

7. **sing perfectly / singer**
   A: What do you think of Joe, Sumi?
   B: I think she _____ in the world.

8. **dance beautifully / dancer**
   A: What do you think of Kang, Sujin?
   B: I think she _____ in Korea.

3 CONVERSATION

A Work with a partner. Fill in the blanks and practice the conversation.

A: How cute is a Siamese cat?
B: It's **one of the cutest** of all cats.

A: How dangerous are black mambas?
B: They're **one of the most dangerous** snakes in Africa.

1 expensive
A: How expensive is a golden retriever?
B: It's _____ of all dogs.

2 rare
A: How rare are pandas?
B: They're _____ animals in the world.

3 fast
A: How fast is a cheetah?
B: It's _____ of all land animals.

4 big
A: How big are anacondas?
B: They're _____ snakes in the world.

▶ Now you are on your own. Ask and answer questions with your partner about the kind of pet in the box below using *one of the most[-est]*.

A: How **strong** is a **grizzly bear**?
B: It's **one of the strongest** animals in the whole world.

- a dolphin / friendly
- a giraffe / tall
- a deer / weak
- a sloth / slow
- a rhinoceros / rare
- cobras / poisonous
- hyenas / fierce
- chimpanzees / smart
- jelly fish / dangerous
- peacocks / splendid

B Work with a partner. Fill in the blanks and practice the conversation.

> **beagles / hyperactive / spaniels**
>
> A: What do you think of **beagles** as a pet?
> B: I hear they're very **hyperactive**.
> A: Are they **more hyperactive** than **spaniels**?
> B: I'm sure they are. I think they are **the most hyperactive** pets of all.

1. **lizards / stinky / snakes**

   A: What do you think of _____ as a pet?
   B: I hear they're very _____.
   A: Are they _____ than _____?
   B: I'm sure they are. I think they are _____ pets of all.

2. **porcupines / tidy / cats**

   A: What do you think of _____ as a pet?
   B: I hear they're very _____.
   A: Are they _____ than _____?
   B: I'm sure they are. I think they are _____ pets of all.

3. **rabbits / gentle / hamsters**

   A: What do you think of _____ as a pet?
   B: I hear they're very _____.
   A: Are they _____ than _____?
   B: I'm sure they are. I think they are _____ pets of all.

▶ Now you are on your own. Talk to your partner about the kinds of pets you've always wanted to have.

A: What do you think of **hamsters** as a pet?
B: I hear they are very **cute**.
A: Are they **cuter** than **squirrels**?
B: I'm sure they are. I think they are the cutest pets of all.

- sharks / hard to take care of / dolphins
- eagles / dangerous / hawks
- goldfish / boring / tropical fish
- parrots / fun / canary
- pigs / smart / dogs
- ferrets / messy / squirrels
- iguanas / hard to feed / snakes
- snails / quiet / turtles

C Work with a partner. Fill in the blanks and practice the conversation.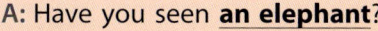

> A: Have you seen **an elephant**?
> B: Yes, I have. I have never seen **such a big** animal in my life.
> A: That's right. **The elephant is the biggest** animal I've ever seen.

1 lion / scary

A: Have you seen _____?
B: Yes, I have. I have never seen _____ animal in my life.
A: That's right. _____ animal I've ever seen.

2 shark / dangerous

A: Have you seen _____?
B: Yes, I have. I have never seen _____ animal in my life.
A: That's right. _____ animal I've ever seen.

3 prairie dog / funny

A: Have you seen _____?
B: Yes, I have. I have never seen _____ animal in my life.
A: That's right. _____ animal I've ever seen.

▶ Work with a partner. Suppose you and your friends are at a zoo or at a pet shop. Have a conversation using the model conversation below.

A: Look at **the puppies**! They are so cute.
B: You are right! They must be the **cutest animals** I've ever seen.

Animals

seals	tigers	wolves
leopards	dolphins	kangaroos
koalas	kittens	alligators
bears	monkeys	parrots
snakes	sloths	

Adjectives

smart	cute	filthy
beautiful	amazing	fast
slow	fierce	scary
big	slim	cool
fat	adorable	funny
creepy	lovely	terrible
ugly	relaxed	

Unit 5

Out to the world with Mr. Moon!

READING & WRITING
Read the passage below and answer the questions.

What is the toughest animal of all? What do you think it is? Maybe a lion? Or a tiger? Or one of the biggest animals like elephants or whales? But scientists would say you are wrong. They say the toughest animal on this planet is the cockroach. The cockroach has existed since the early stages of evolution, and it has lasted for hundreds of thousands of years. It can survive in the harshest living environments in all kinds of climates because it can live for years without eating anything. And it can even survive in outer space. Scientists also say that it might be the last to survive on the earth when all other species go extinct. That's right. It is the toughest animal on earth. And it will be the last one standing.

1. What did you think the toughest animal of all was?
➔

2. What is the toughest animal on the earth according to scientists?
➔

3. Since when have cockroaches existed?
➔

4. Why can they survive in all living environments?
➔

5. Can they survive in outer space?
➔

WRITING

Do you have a pet now? Or have you ever had any pet? Tell me about your pets. Write down why you like them or you don't like them.

I have two dogs and two cats.

Actually, they're not just pets but my family.

Unit 6

What Do You Plan to Do on the Weekend?

LESSON PLAN

1. Topic
- Plans and Appointments

2. Function
- Talking about Planning for the Future
- Arranging and Rearranging of Appointments

3. Grammar
- Will / Be Going to / Plan to + Base verb

1. What are you going to do now[today, tonight]?
2. Do you have a plan for the weekend[the vacation, summer, winter]?
3. What do you plan to do?
4. When do you usually meet people?
5. Why do you usually meet people? For pleasure or for business?
6. How do you make an appointment?
7. How do you cancel an appointment?

Unit 6 What do you plan to do on the weekend?

1 WORDS & EXPRESSIONS

1. visit our ancestors' graves
2. family reunion
3. rest in a pedicure salon
4. go on a company excursion
5. do research at the library
6. work overtime
7. take a day off from work
8. attend a meeting
9. work in the family's restaurant
10. be out of town on business
11. go to a year-end party
12. hang out with
13. go to the midnight show
14. go on a blind date
15. clean out the refrigerator
16. visit one's in-laws
17. hook up one's computer
18. take back library books
19. relax at home
20. catch up with
21. go out with
22. string up one's Christmas decorations
23. go to the beauty parlor for a perm

2 GRAMMAR

Future (Will / Be Going to / Plan to + Base verb)	
Positives	Positive Questions
I plan to visit Jim.	Do I plan to visit Jim?
You plan to visit Jim.	Do you plan to visit Jim?
He plans to visit Jim.	Does he plan to visit Jim?
She plans to visit Jim.	Does she plan to visit Jim?
We plan to visit Jim.	Do we plan to visit Jim?
They plan to visit Jim.	Do they plan to visit Jim?
Negatives	WH-Questions
I don't plan to visit Jim.	What do I plan to do today?
You don't plan to visit Jim.	What do you plan to do today?
He doesn't plan to visit Jim.	What does he plan to do today?
She doesn't plan to visit Jim.	What does she plan to do today?
We don't plan to visit Jim.	What do we plan to do today?
They don't plan to visit Jim.	What do they plan to do today?

A Fill in the blanks.

A: Are you going to have a night out with your colleagues tonight?
B: Yes, **I am**. **I'm going to have a night out with my colleagues.**

A: Will you visit your in-laws tomorrow?
B: Yes, **I will**. **I will visit my in-laws.**

1. A: Is Andrew going to go to the movies this afternoon?
B: Yes, _____.
_____

2. A: Are Jenny's parents going to celebrate their wedding anniversary next Saturday?
B: Yes, _____.
_____

3. A: Is the train going to arrive in a few minutes?
B: Yes, _____.
_____

4. A: Will your grandma plant flowers in the garden this summer?
B: Yes, _____.
_____

5. A: Are you and your friends going to go hiking in the mountains today?
B: Yes, _____.
_____

6. A: Will Amanda work in the family's restaurant from September?
B: Yes, _____.
_____

7. A: Is Jerry going to leave the office soon?
B: Yes, _____.
_____

B Fill in the blanks with the appropriate expressions.

A: What **do you plan to do** for the weekend?
B: I **plan to do the household chores**.

1. **Joe / travel the east coast**

   A: What _____ for the summer vacation?

   B: He _____.

2. **your children / go to ski camp**

   A: What _____ for the winter vacation?

   B: They _____.

3. **Tess / buy presents for her family at the mall**

   A: What _____ for the Christmas season?

   B: She _____.

4. **you and your family / visit our ancestors' graves**

   A: What _____ for the Chuseok holiday?

   B: We _____.

5. **Angie / rest in a pedicure salon**

   A: What _____ for this Saturday?

   B: She _____.

6. **Mark / go to his hometown for a family reunion**

   A: What _____ for lunar New Year's Day?

   B: He _____.

7. **Mr. and Mrs. Williams / cook sweet and sour pork together**

   A: What _____ for today?

   B: They _____.

3 CONVERSATION

A Work with a partner. Fill in the blanks and practice the conversation.

> A: **Do you have any plan** for tonight?
> B: Let me see. I think I'm going to **go see a movie**.

> A: **Do you have any plan** for tomorrow?
> B: Let me see. I think I'll **go on a company excursion**.

1 your son / go out with Helen

A: _____ for tonight?

B: Let me see. I think he's going to _____.

2 your daughter / do research at the library

A: _____ for tomorrow?

B: Let me see. I think she'll _____.

3 Dave / work overtime

A: _____ for tonight?

B: Let me see. I think he's going to _____.

▶ Now you are on your own. Practice the conversation below with your partner. Use *be going to* or *will*.

A: Do you have any plan for tonight?
B: Let me see. I think I'm going to **hang out with my friends**.

A: Do you have any plan for tomorrow?
B: Let me see. I think I'll **attend 5 meetings in a row** tomorrow.

- go to a year-end party
- watch movies on the computer
- work with my team at a café
- have a drink
- go to the midnight show
- go to the sauna and get a massage
- have a good night's sleep
- have a midnight snack with my roommate

- relax at home
- go bowling
- go out with my boyfriend[girlfriend]
- have a meeting with my clients
- take a day off from work
- clean out the refrigerator
- hook up my new computer
- string up the Christmas decorations

Unit 6 63

B Work with a partner. Fill in the blanks and practice the conversation.

A: Shall we have a good time tomorrow?
B: I'd love to. But I'm afraid I'll have to **finish my report**.
A: What about the day after tomorrow?
B: Well, I'm supposed to **go to church**. Sorry.

1. **go to the dentist / go to the beauty parlor for a perm**

   A: Shall we have a good time tomorrow?
   B: I'd love to. But I'm afraid I'll have to _____.
   A: What about the day after tomorrow?
   B: Well, I'm supposed to _____. Sorry.

2. **work overtime / be out of town on business**

   A: Shall we have a good time tomorrow?
   B: I'd love to. But I'm afraid I'll have to _____.
   A: What about the day after tomorrow?
   B: Well, I'm supposed to _____. Sorry.

▶ Now you are on your own. You and your partner are making an appointment. Try to adjust the time and place for the meeting.

A: Shall we meet **on Saturday**?
B: Well, I'm supposed to **see my aunt** on Saturday. How about on Sunday?
A: Sunday is good for me. Where shall we meet?
B: What about meeting **at the school gate**?
A: That would be great!

- on Monday[Tuesday, Wednesday, Thursday, Friday, Saturday, Sunday]
- at noon[midnight, dawn]
- in the morning[evening]

- attend a class
- clean out the closet
- meet with my clients

- feed my cat
- see a dentist
- take back my library books

- at the bus stop[park, airport, bank, café, church, restaurant, shopping mall, bakery]

64 English Fly High | Speeding

C Work with a partner. Fill in the blanks and practice the conversation. 🎧 17

> A: Do you have any plan for **tonight**?
> B: I thought I was going to **catch up with my work**. Why?
> A: Well, I thought you might want to **go for a beer**.
> B: Hmm. I will think about changing my plans then.

1. **this month / start studying Chinese / learn some Japanese with me**

   A: Do you have any plan for _____?

   B: I thought I was going to _____. Why?

   A: Well, I thought you might want to _____.

   B: Hmm. I will think about changing my plans then.

2. **this weekend / clean the whole house / go on a blind date with one of my female friends**

   A: Do you have any plan for _____?

   B: I thought I was going to _____. Why?

   A: Well, I thought you might want to _____.

   B: Hmm. I will think about changing my plans then.

▶ Work with a partner. Suppose you are going to meet your business partner-to-be who is a total stranger to you. Fix the things below through a phone call using the model conversation below.

A: What is an appropriate date and time for you?
B: 3 o'clock Monday, the 23rd, would be good for me.
A: How about 4 o'clock Thursday, the 26th?
B: That's okay for me, too.
A: Where shall we meet, then?
B: How about meeting at my office?
A: OK, I'll be there on time.

Place

at the lobby of my building, at the front gate, at City Hall plaza, at Starbucks, at the Hilton hotel, at Seoul Station, at the restaurant near your office, in Shinchon, in Myeongdong

Out to the world with Mr. Moon!

READING & WRITING
Read the passage below and answer the questions.

I have been to the sea for vacation all my life. But I couldn't spend my vacation at the beach this summer. I was severely ill and got an operation on my stomach. My family members were worried about me because I couldn't get out of bed for a long time. But I got back on my feet again this week. I'm healthy now. So now I am full of hope that I can go to the ocean again. I am going to enjoy sunbathing at the beach. I am going to have a drink in my hand and lie down with the burning sand on my back. I am going to swim in the sea and feel the waves wash over my healthy body. I am going to go to some beach parties with my friends, too. All in all, I am sure this vacation trip will be the best and the happiest one of all because I feel like I am born again!

1. Where has the writer been for vacation all his life?
→

2. Why couldn't he spend his vacation at the beach this summer?
→

3. When did he get back on his feet?
→

4. What hopes does he have now after he became healthy?
→

5. Why is he sure that this vacation will be the best one?
→

WRITING

What were your plans for this year? Were they accomplished? And do you have any plans for next year? Write down your past and future plans.

I was going to learn how to play the guitar this year.

Unit 7

By Whom Was the Speech Delivered?

LESSON PLAN

1 Topic
- School[College]

2 Function
- Talking about School[College] Life
- Memories on Younger Years in School

3 Grammar
- Passive Voice
- Passive with Various Tenses: Passive Negatives, Passive Questions, WH-Questions

1. What major was studied by you in college?
2. What club activities were taken part in by you when you were a student?
3. What were you interested in most when you were in high school?
4. Was there anyone who was picked on by classmates?
5. Which teacher was liked the best by you?
6. Which subject was liked the best by you?

Unit 7 — By whom was the speech delivered?

1 WORDS & EXPRESSIONS

1 janitor	2 auditorium	3 laboratory	4 midterm
5 physics	6 philosophy	7 deadline	8 principal
9 submit	10 provide	11 elect	12 get better grades
13 take a course	14 practice *karate*	15 play squash	16 take out
17 substitute with	18 take away	19 school committee	20 look after
21 pick on	22 put away	23 donate	24 laugh at
25 look down on	26 take part in	27 newly	
28 put in the equipment		29 throw away the books	
30 musical instrument		31 give a presentation	
32 extend one's gratitude		33 do the survey	
34 turn on[off] the computer		35 put off the schedule	

2 GRAMMAR

Passive Voice (Be verb + Past Participle)		
Active	**Passive**	**Passive Questions**
I saw him.	He was seen by me.	Was he seen by me?
You kissed her.	She was kissed by you.	Was she kissed by you?
He played it.	It was played by him.	Was it played by him?
She hurt me.	I was hurt by her.	Was I hurt by her?
It helped them.	They were helped by it.	Were they helped by it?
They ate kimchi.	Kimchi was eaten by them.	Was kimchi eaten by them?
We killed the bear.	The bear was killed by us.	Was the bear killed by us?
Passive Negatives		**WH-Questions**
He wasn't seen by me.		Who was seen by me?
She wasn't kissed by you.		Who was kissed by you?
It wasn't played by him.		What was played by him?
I wasn't hurt by her.		Who was hurt by her?
They weren't helped by it.		Who were helped by it?
Kimchi wasn't eaten by them.		What was eaten by them?
The bear wasn't killed by us.		What was killed by us?

70 English Fly High | Speeding

A Fill in the blanks changing the active voice into a passive one.

A: She takes a physics course this semester.
B: A physics course **is taken by her this semester**.

A: Mr. Moon taught Unit 6 today.
B: Unit 6 **was taught by Mr. Moon today**.

1. A: The teachers cared about their students.
   B: Their students _____.

2. A: They practice *karate* in gym class.
   B: *Karate* _____.

3. A: Nancy solved the mathematics problem at last.
   B: The mathematics problem _____.

4. A: Matthew plays the flute in the school orchestra.
   B: The flute _____.

5. A: I made a book club with my classmates.
   B: A book club _____.

6. A: Students eat lunch in the school cafeteria every day.
   B: Lunch _____.

7. A: Jenny and her friends play squash after school.
   B: Squash _____.

B Fill in the blanks and change the sentence into a passive voice.

A: I will get better grades for my midterms.
B: Better grades **will be gotten by me for my midterms**.

A: Mr. Cooper is going to send an e-mail in advance.
B: An e-mail **is going to be sent in advance by Mr. Cooper**.

1. A: She will take a physics course next semester.

   B: A physics course _____.

2. A: I'm not going to forget the deadline for reports.

   B: The deadline for reports _____.

3. A: Charlie will learn essay writing with his friends.

   B: Essay writing _____.

4. A: We're going to hold a graduation party in December.

   B: A graduation party _____.

5. A: Mark is going to do volunteer work this winter vacation.

   B: Volunteer work _____.

6. A: You won't eat a dessert after dinner.

   B: A dessert _____.

7. A: Linda is going to buy a leather jacket.

   B: A leather jacket _____.

3 CONVERSATION

A Work with a partner. Fill in the blanks and practice the conversation.

Did Beethoven compose our school song?

A: Was our school song **composed by Beethoven**?
B: No, **it wasn't composed by Beethoven**.

Has the school committee resolved the serious problem?

A: Has the serious problem **been resolved by the school committee**?
B: Yes, **it has been resolved by the school committee**.

① Will they elect Brenda as a student leader this time?

A: Will Brenda _____?
B: Yes, _____.

② Did the students use iPads in their class?

A: Were iPads _____?
B: No, _____.

▶ Now you are on your own. Talk to your partner about by whom was some work done. Ask and answer questions like the model conversations.

Did the school janitor fix the broken lights?

A: Were the broken lights fixed by the school janitor?
B: Yes, they were fixed by the school janitor. / No, they weren't fixed by the school janitor.

Has Mary given a presentation in the social studies class?

A: Has a presentation been given in the social studies class by Mary?
B: Yes, it has been given in the social studies class by Mary. /
   No, it hasn't been given in the social studies class by Mary.

- Do students clean the classroom?
- Can you substitute the test with a paper?
- Will the high school build a new school auditorium?
- Did the college renovate the laboratory?
- Has the school never accepted cheating?
- Does Meg take private lessons after school?
- Will they support various after-school programs?
- Are we going to elect the president of our class today?

B Work with a partner. Fill in the blanks and practice the conversation.

> A: Did you take away my umbrella?
> B: No, it **wasn't taken away by me**.
> A: By whom **was it taken away** then?
> B: It **was taken away by Sam**.

1. **Professor Tang**
   A: Did Professor Wilson take out math from the list?
   B: No, it _____.
   A: By whom _____ then?
   B: It _____.

2. **the principal**
   A: Did Mandy put off the party date?
   B: No, it _____.
   A: By whom _____ then?
   B: It _____.

3. **Mrs. Parker**
   A: Does Mrs. Black take care of sick students today?
   B: No, they _____.
   A: By whom _____ then?
   B: They _____.

▶ Now you are on your own. You and your partner are trying to find the person who did the following things. Using the model conversation to practice the passive voice.

A: Did you turn on the computer?
B: No, it **wasn't turned on by me**.
A: By whom **was it turned on** then?
B: It **was turned on** by John.

- turn on[off] the computers
- put off the schedule
- put in the equipment
- laugh at my brother
- pick on my sister

- put on[take off] the sweater
- put away the toys
- throw away the books
- look down on Jason
- look after Adrian

C Work with a partner. Fill in the blanks and practice the conversation.

> A: Who will do the PPT part?
> B: I think it **will be done** by Sarah.
> A: Who **did** the PPT part last time?
> B: Hmm. It was Suzuki. It **was done** by Suzuki.

1 A: Who is going to ring the bell?
B: I think it _____ by Josh.
A: Who _____ the bell last time?
B: Hmm. It was Susan. It _____ by Susan.

2 A: Who will read this philosophy book?
B: I think it _____ by Sam.
A: Who _____ this book last time?
B: Hmm. It was Jennifer. It _____ by Jennifer.

3 A: Who is going to sing the song at a school talent show?
B: I think it _____ by Cathy.
A: Who _____ the song last time?
B: Hmm. It was Jim. It _____ by Jim.

▶ Work with a partner. Form a group of 3 or 4. You are a team which is going to give a presentation on some subject in front of the class. Try to decide who is going to do which part and report it to the class.

A: Who will[is going to] **do the survey**?
B: I think it should be done by Tim.
A: Then what about **giving the presentation**?
B: I think it should be given by Samantha.

- write the report
- print the paper and pass out to the class
- submit it to the teacher
- design the PPT file

Out to the world with Mr. Moon!

READING & WRITING
Read the passage below and answer the questions.

Hi, everyone,

I am Sam Walters, principal of the newly found New Orleans Jazz High School. First of all, I'd like to extend my deepest gratitude to all those people who took part in founding this wonderful school by helping and generously giving what they have with warm hearts. The school building was donated by Mr. Anderson, president of the New Orleans Contractors' Society. The musical instruments were given by the New Orleans Yamaha factory. And the school furniture was provided by the local IKEA branch. The books in the library were rented with no limits by Amazon, the internet enterprise. Most of all, smartphones in the hands of all the NOJH students were given by Apple. With all this amazing help from the community, I firmly believe that world class musical achievements will eventually be made by the students of this school. This is a school that was not found by just one person or one organization. It was built by everyone who has a passionate heart for Jazz music in New Orleans.

1. What kind of school do you think it is?
→

2. By whom was the school building donated?
→

3. By what factory were the musical instruments given?
→

4. By what branch was the school furniture provided?
→

5. By what company were the students' smartphones given?
→

6. By whom was this school built according to the principal's speech?
→

WRITING

Do you remember the time when you were a high school student or college student? How was it? Write down about your school life using the expressions you have learned from this unit.

My teacher, Mr. Moon was looked up to by a lot of students.

English was taught by him.

Unit 8

Flowers Were Given to Me Every Day by You.

LESSON PLAN

1) Topic
- Celebrations and Anniversaries

2) Function
- Talking about Presents
- Talking about Activities Celebrating Anniversaries and Holidays

3) Grammar
- Passive Voice:
Be + P.P. + D.O. /
Be + P.P. + to, for, of + I.O.

1. When were you born?
2. How was your last birthday celebrated?
3. What present was given to you on your birthday?
4. What are your special days and anniversaries?
5. What is usually done on those days by you?
6. What will be done on the next holiday by you?

Unit 8 Flowers were given to me every day by you.

1 WORDS & EXPRESSIONS

1 bring	2 offer	3 issue
4 award	5 deliver	6 grant
7 necklace	8 comfort	9 kite
10 mob	11 quota	12 be tired of
13 happiness	14 permission	15 the U.S. embassy
16 wedding cake	17 scholarship	18 Lamborghini
19 internship	20 foundation	21 allotment
22 payout	23 New Year's Day	24 farewell party
25 Thanksgiving Day	26 Halloween costumes	27 Valentine dinner
28 be interested in	29 be disappointed with	30 be known to
31 be bored with	32 be pleased with	33 be satisfied with
34 be surprised at	35 be filled with	36 be worried about
37 be dressed in		

2 GRAMMAR

Passive Voice (Be + P.P. + D.O. / Be + P.P. + to, for, of + I.O.)			
	Active	Passive 1	Passive 2
Positives	I gave her flowers.	She was given flowers by me.	Flowers were given to her by me.
Questions	Did I give her flowers?	Was she given flowers by me?	Were flowers given to her by me?
Negatives	I didn't give her flowers.	She wasn't given flowers by me.	Flowers weren't given to her by me.
Negative Questions	Didn't I give her flowers?	Wasn't she given flowers by me?	Weren't flowers given to her by me?
WH-Questions	Whom did I give flowers to? What did I give her?	Who was given flowers by me?	What were given to her by me?

80 English Fly High | Speeding

A Fill in the blanks changing the active voice into a passive one.

for me	A: She makes me a cake on my birthday.
	B: I am made a cake on my birthday by her. (X)
	A cake **is made for me on my birthday by her**. (O)

1. **for his wife**
   A: Henry bought his wife a beautiful necklace.
   B: A beautiful necklace _____.

2. **to us**
   A: Music brings us comfort and happiness.
   B: Comfort and happiness _____.

3. **to Ralph**
   A: Gina wrote Ralph a birthday card yesterday.
   B: A birthday card _____.

4. **to me**
   A: She always sells me turkey for half price on Thanksgiving Day.
   B: Turkey _____.

5. **for him**
   A: His grandfather made him a nice kite last New Year's Day.
   B: A Nice kite _____.

6. **for us**
   A: Ginger cooked us a nice Valentine dinner.
   B: A nice Valentine dinner _____.

7. **to people**
   A: The convenience store sold people a lot of candies and chocolate.
   B: A lot of candies and chocolate _____.

8. **to my mom**
   A: My dad still writes my mom love letters once a week.
   B: Love letters _____.

B Fill in the blanks and change the sentence into a passive one.

to me
A: Dad will send me a Barbie doll for Christmas.
B: I **will be sent a Barbie doll for Christmas by Dad**. (O)
   A Barbie doll **will be sent to me for Christmas by Dad**. (O)

1. **to Eve**

   A: Adam gives Eve flowers every day.

   B: Eve _____.

   Flowers _____.

2. **to him**

   A: A lot of fans offered him presents and love letters.

   B: He _____.

   Presents and love letters _____.

3. **to students**

   A: Mr. Cruise taught his students many songs.

   B: His students _____.

   Many songs _____.

4. **for Sandra**

   A: Molly is going to find Sandra a job.

   B: Sandra _____.

   A job _____.

5. **of his friends**

   A: James asked his friends questions about Halloween costumes.

   B: His friends _____.

   Questions _____.

6. **to her children**

   A: Amy told her children the story of Santa Claus.

   B: Her children _____.

   The story of Santa Claus _____.

3 CONVERSATION

A Work with a partner. Fill in the blanks and practice the conversation.

to her
A: Did John show Lillian his house?
B: That's right. His house **was shown to her by John**.
A: You mean she **was shown his house by John**?
B: Yes, **she was**!

1 to him
A: Did the U.S. embassy issue him a visa?
B: That's right. A visa _____.
A: You mean he _____?
B: Yes, _____!

2 to me
A: Did Martha tell you his secret?
B: That's right. His secret _____.
A: You mean you _____?
B: Yes, _____!

▶ Now you are on your own. Suppose your partner is a person who exaggerates everything. And you can't take his word for it. So, you want to check everything he says by asking questions. Use passive sentences and practice the conversation below.

A: You know what? **I was offered a scholarship by Harvard.**
B: I can't believe it! **You were offered a scholarship by Harvard?**
A: That's right! **Harvard offered me a scholarship!**
B: You're joking, right? **A scholarship was offered to you by Harvard.** Really?
A: No, I'm just kidding. Ha, ha, ha.

- I was proposed to by Clark.
- I was sent a hundred roses on my birthday by Dave.
- I was given a Lamborghini by my dad.
- I was shown her year book pictures by Liz.
- I was lent 4 million dollars by one of my friends.
- I was found a lot of gold bars by my dog.
- I was given a diamond ring by my husband.
- I was told something surprising about his past by Jules.
- I was sent an invitation for lunch by Warren Buffet.
- I was paid a huge salary by Apple.

Unit 8 83

B Work with a partner. Fill in the blanks and practice the conversation 🎧22

> A: Were you promised an internship by the company?
> B: No, **I wasn't**. Nothing **was promised to you by the company**.

> A: You mean **you weren't promised an internship by the company**?
> B: No. It seems you've heard something wrong.

① A: Was Pitt granted permission by the government?

B: No, _____. Nothing _____.

A: You mean _____?

B: No. It seems you've heard something wrong.

② A: Was Jessica given a surprise farewell party by her colleagues?

B: No, _____. Nothing _____.

A: You mean _____?

B: No. It seems you've heard something wrong.

③ A: Were you and Don awarded a $10,000 prize by the foundation?

B: No, _____. Nothing _____.

A: You mean _____?

B: No. It seems you've heard something wrong.

▶ Now you are on your own. Suppose you've heard some rumor about someone you know and try to confirm it to your partner with passive sentences. Use the model conversation.

> A: I hear that **Lee, Byunghun was offered a role as 007 from Hollywood**.
> B: You must be mistaken. He wasn't offered anything as far as I know.
> A: Wasn't he offered anything from Hollywood?
> B: Nothing was offered to him. I'm positive.

- your professor was delivered a bomb by one of his students
- Kong, Hodong was taught English by Mr. Moon
- Mark was handed a gun by a mob member
- Patty's husband was given a large payout by the insurance company
- Diane was found her lost jewels by the vacuum cleaner

C Work with a partner. Fill in the blanks and practice the conversation. 🎧 23

> **be known to**
>
> A: Everybody in China knows his name.
> B: Are you sure **his name is known to** everybody in China?
> A: Certainly. **His name is really known to everybody in China.**

1. **be interested in**

   A: The big yellow rubber duck will interest all the people.

   B: Are you sure _____ the big yellow rubber duck?

   A: Certainly. _____

2. **be covered with**

   A: White chocolate covered the top of the wedding cake.

   B: Are you sure _____ white chocolate?

   A: Certainly. _____

3. **be surprised at**

   A: Robin's gift is going to surprise Molly.

   B: Are you sure _____ Robin's gift?

   A: Certainly. _____

▶ Work with a partner. Suppose you have been to a party and you are talking about how the party was with your friends. About what you wore, who you met, what you ate, and so on. Practice the conversation below using the passive voice.

> A: How was the party yesterday?
> B: I **was bored with** the same people and the same subjects.
> A: Were you really bored with the same people and the same subjects?
> B: Certainly. I was really bored with them.

- be disappointed with
- be surprised at
- be worried about
- be pleased with
- be known to
- be satisfied with
- be tired of
- be dressed in
- be interested in
- be filled with

Unit 8 85

Out to the world with Mr. Moon!

READING & WRITING
Read the passage below and answer the questions.

Sam is happiest when he sees his wife happy after she is given presents by him. Not only on her birthday or on their anniversaries, but also on an average day, he always thinks of buying her stuff. However, Sandy, his wife, doesn't want to be given a lot of presents by Sam. Not that she doesn't enjoy the idea of being given gifts from Sam, but she thinks that too much money is spent on buying her stuff by Sam. So "a gift quota" was offered to Sam by Sandy. It's an allotment of money allowed to be spent for the month. Usually the quota is as much as 100 dollars a month. But, for December, 300 dollars are promised to Sam by her because Christmas holidays are just around the corner. If there was a medal awarded to cute and lovely couples, it would surely be given to Sam and Sandy.

1. When is Sam happiest?
→

2. What does Sam always think of?
→

3. Why doesn't Sandy want to be given a lot of presents by Sam?
→

4. What was offered to Sam by his wife?
→

5. What is a gift quota?
→

6. How much is promised to Sam as a gift quota for December by his wife?
→

WRITING

What are your special days and anniversaries? And when are they? What did you do on those days this year? Write down how you celebrated your birthday and anniversaries using the expressions you have learned from this unit.

I was given a hundred roses on my birthday by my boyfriend.

Unit 9

What Is the Price of Your New Smartphone?

LESSON PLAN

① Topic
- Numbers: Under 1,000,000

② Function
- Talking with Numbers: Under 1,000,000
- Talking about Prices
- Talking about One's Expenses

③ Grammar
- Counting Numbers: Under 1,000,000
- To Infinitive (As a Subjective Complement)

1. How much is your jacket[cardigan, skirt, etc.]?
2. How much is your tumbler[pencil case, wallet, etc.]?
3. How much did your digital devices[cell phone, laptop, watch, etc.] cost?
4. How much do you get paid for your part-time job?
5. What was the price of the item you have bought recently?
6. What is the salary range you want to get paid?

Unit 9 What is the price of your new smartphone?

1 WORDS & EXPRESSIONS

1. cardigan
2. plaid shirt
3. running shoes
4. bracelet
5. striped blouse
6. tennis shorts
7. leather boots
8. wallet
9. duck down parka
10. backpack
11. washing machine
12. suitcase
13. chopsticks
14. water purifier
15. cooker
16. tablet
17. microwave oven
18. digital camera
19. plasma screen TV
20. laptop
21. part-time work
22. guard
23. celebrity
24. cost
25. glamorous
26. spending
27. organic
28. thrifty

2 GRAMMAR

Numbers under 1,000,000 (a million)			
1,000		10,000	
1,000	one thousand	10,000	ten thousand
2,000	two thousand	20,000	twenty thousand
3,000	three thousand	30,000	thirty thousand
4,500	four thousand, five hundred	45,000	forty-five thousand
6,780	six thousand, seven hundred (and) eighty	67,800	sixty-seven thousand, eight hundred
100,000			
100,000	A hundred thousand		
200,000	two hundred thousand		
300,000	three hundred thousand		
450,000	four hundred fifty thousand		
678,000	six hundred (and) seventy-eight thousand		

- **To Infinitive (as a subjective complement)**: My job is **to wait on tables**. (My job = to wait on tables)

A Write down the numbers in the blanks as shown below.

50,000 won
A: How much did you pay for your cardigan?
B: I paid **fifty thousand won**.

1. **12,000 won**
   A: How much did you pay for this yellow hat?
   B: I paid _____.

2. **95,000 won**
   A: How much did you pay for the sunglasses?
   B: I paid _____.

3. **38,900 won**
   A: How much did you pay for your nice backpack?
   B: I paid _____.

4. **19,900 won**
   A: How much did you pay for your plaid shirt?
   B: I paid _____.

5. **45,000 won**
   A: How much did you pay for the white chair?
   B: I paid _____.

6. **58,930 won**
   A: How much did you pay for the black wallet?
   B: I paid _____.

7. **100,050 won**
   A: How much did you pay for your organic shampoo?
   B: I paid _____.

B Write down the numbers in the blanks as shown.

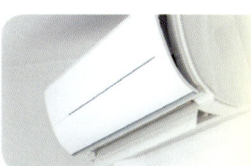

A: How much did it cost you to buy an air conditioner?

B: It cost me a lot **more[less] than seven hundred thousand** won.

1. **more than 600,000**

   A: How much did it cost you to buy a washing machine?

   B: It cost me a lot _____ won.

2. **less than 100,000**

   A: How much did it cost you to buy a microwave oven?

   B: It cost me a lot _____ won.

3. **more than 800,000**

   A: How much did it cost you to buy a refrigerator?

   B: It cost me a lot _____ won.

4. **less than 300,000**

   A: How much did it cost you to buy an electric cooker?

   B: It cost me a lot _____ won.

5. **more than 400,000**

   A: How much did it cost to buy a water purifier?

   B: It cost me a lot _____ won.

6. **less than 200,000**

   A: How much did it cost you to buy a vacuum cleaner?

   B: It cost me a lot _____ won.

7. **more than 900,000**

   A: How much did it cost you to buy a plasma screen TV?

   B: It cost me a lot _____ won.

3 CONVERSATION

A Work with a partner. Fill in the blanks and practice the conversation.

220,000 won
A: I'm looking for a gold ring.
B: How about **this one** over here.
A: Ok, I'll take **that one**. How much **is it**?
B: **It's two hundred (and) twenty thousand won.**

350,000 won
A: I'm looking for sneakers.
B: How about **these ones** over here.
A: Ok, I'll take **those ones**. How much **are they**?
B: **They're three hundred (and) fifty thousand won.**

① 136,000 won

A: I'm looking for a striped blouse.
B: How about _____ over here.
A: Ok, I'll take _____. How much _____?
B: _____

② 320,000 won

A: I'm looking for a pair of earrings.
B: How about _____ over here.
A: Ok, I'll take _____. How much _____?
B: _____

▶ Suppose you are shopping at a shopping mall and you want to buy clothes, personal items or electronic goods under 900,000 won worth. Your partner is the clerk at the store. Have a shopping conversation as below.

A: May I help you?
B: I'm looking for **a pair of jeans**.
A: How about **these ones** over here.
B: Ok, I'll take **those ones**. How much are they?
A: **They're one hundred sixty thousand won.**

- a pair of slippers / 9,900 won
- a pair of tennis shorts / 89,000 won
- a pair of running shoes / 159,000 won
- a pair of thick socks / 3,580 won
- a pair of trousers / 78,000 won
- a pair of scissors / 13,200 won
- a pair of sandals / 64,000 won
- a pair of black sunglasses / 260,000 won
- a pair of gloves / 35,000 won
- a pair of chopsticks / 12,700 won

Unit 9 93

B Work with a partner. Fill in the blanks and practice the conversation.

> **a waitress / wait on table / 500,000**
> A: What do you do for part-time work?
> B: **I work as a waitress and my job is to wait on tables.**
> A: How much do you get paid there?
> B: **I get paid five hundred thousand** won per month.

1. **a guard / keep watch at the bank / 700,000**

   A: What does your brother do for part-time work?
   B: _____
   A: How much does he get paid there?
   B: _____ won per month.

2. **dish washers / wash the dishes at the restaurant / 350,000**

   A: What do Mark and Anthony do for part-time work?
   B: _____
   A: How much do they get paid there?
   B: _____ won per month.

▶ Now you are on your own. Suppose you are having a job interview for part-time work at a company. Ask and answer questions about the work conditions.

> A: What's my job?
> B: Your job is **to cook bread**.
> A: How much will I get paid an hour?
> B: You will get paid **six thousand** won an hour.
>
> A: What's the total amount of money for a month?
> B: That will be **six hundred thousand** won.

- teach students English / 10,000 / 800,000
- park customer's cars at the parking lot / 7,000 / 665,000
- give private lessons to high school students / 6,000 / 330,000
- deliver pizza / 6,500 / 455,000
- take care of babies / 7,000 / 560,000
- wash the windows of buildings / 8,000 / 720,000
- feed penguins at the zoo / 10,000 / 990,000
- serve customers at the restaurant / 8,500 / 897,500

C Work with a partner. Fill in the blanks and practice the conversation. 🎧26

> **shoes / 176,000 won**
>
> A: Wow, your new **shoes look** very expensive.
> B: Well, **they weren't** very cheap.
> A: What was the price of **the shoes**?
> B: It was **a hundred and seventy-six thousand**. I worked part-time to pay for **them**.

1. **duck down parka / 436,000 won**

    A: Wow, your new _____ very expensive.
    B: Well, _____ very cheap.
    A: What was the price of _____?
    B: It was _____.
       I worked part-time to pay for _____.

2. **leather boots / 238,000 won**

    A: Wow, your new _____ very expensive.
    B: Well, _____ very cheap.
    A: What was the price of _____?
    B: It was _____.
       I worked part-time to pay for _____.

▶ Work with a partner. You are chatting with your friend about the new item that you've just bought. Talk about the price and how you made enough money to buy it.

> **bracelet / 142,000 won**
>
> A: Your new **bracelet looks** brand new.
>   How much did you pay for it?
> B: I paid **a hundred and forty two thousand won for it**.
>   Actually, I paid more than I should have.
> A: Did you work hard to get it?
> B: Of course! I worked part-time for 120 hours a month!

- laptop / 990,000 won
- tablet / 660,000 won
- suitcase / 340,000 won
- headphones / 130,000 won
- digital camera / 536,200 won
- bicycles / 770,000 won
- leather jacket / 898,000 won
- sunglasses / 482,090 won

Unit 9 95

Out to the world with Mr. Moon!

READING & WRITING
Read the passage below and answer the questions.

Kent Harris is a famous actor who leads a glamorous life in the public eye. But his spending habits are unexpectedly thrifty. He has limits on how much he spends for each item that he buys. He doesn't buy shirts more expensive than 40 dollars. When he buys pants, he always buys them under the price of 60 dollars. He doesn't eat meals when the price is higher than 12 dollars, even for dinner. He doesn't spend more than 200 dollars at one time. For every item that he buys, he has limits that are extremely low for a celebrity. But what is more surprising is that these limits only count for how much he spends on himself. He has been donating more than 200,000 dollars per year for the last 10 years. What a lovely star he is!

1. What does Kent do?
→

2. How are his spending habits?
→

3. What is his limit on spending for a shirt?
→

4. What is the price limit for pants when he buys them?
→

5. How much has he been donating per year?
→

WRITING

Is there anything you have bought recently? What did you buy and what was the price? Write down the list of items you bought and their prices using the expressions you have learned from this unit.

1. hairpin : 13,200 (thirteen thousand (and) two hundred) won

Unit 10

How Much Does It Cost to Buy a UHD TV?

LESSON PLAN

① Topic
- Numbers: Above 1,000,000

② Function
- Talking with Numbers: Above 1,000,000
- Explaining Living Expenses
- Talking about Prices of Expensive Things Such as Cars and Houses

③ Grammar
- Counting Numbers: Above 1,000,000
- To Infinitive (As a Noun, an Adjective and an Adverb)

1. How much is your TV[refrigerator, washing machine, etc.]?
2. Tell me about your living expenses: transportation, rent, cosmetics, food, etc.
3. What is the price of your dream car?
4. Do you have enough money to buy your dream car?
5. What is the price of your dream house?
6. Are you doing anything to make your dreams come true?

Unit 10 How much does it cost to buy a UHD TV?

1 WORDS & EXPRESSIONS

1. goods
2. currently
3. out of stock
4. price range
5. approximate price
6. vehicle
7. HD camcorder
8. ice dispenser
9. grand piano
10. synthesizer
11. stereo system
12. steam gas dryer
13. 4-door French refrigerator
14. immigrate
15. capital
16. ball park figure
17. approximately
18. retirement
19. population
20. folk
21. megapolis
22. fur coat
23. refer to
24. found a start-up
25. save
26. achieve the goal
27. lunar New Year's Day

2 GRAMMAR

Numbers above 1,000,000 (a million)				
1,000,000			**10,000,000**	
1,000,000	one million		10,000,000	ten million
2,000,000	two million		20,000,000	twenty million
3,000,000	three million		30,000,000	thirty million
4,500,000	four million, five hundred thousand		45,000,000	forty-five million
6,780,000	six million, seven hundred (and) eighty thousand		67,800,000	sixty-seven million, eight hundred thousand
100,000,000			**1,000,000,000**	
100,000,000	a hundred million		1,000,000,000	one billion
200,000,000	two hundred million		2,000,000,000	two billion
300,000,000	three hundred million		3,000,000,000	three billion
450,000,000	four hundred (and) fifty million		4,500,000,000	four billion, five hundred million
678,000,000	six hundred (and) seventy eight million		6,780,000,000	six billion, seven hundred (and) eighty million

- **To Infinitive** 1) **as a noun** (subject of a clause): How much does it cost **to buy a UHD TV**?
  2) **as an adjective** (a noun modifier): There are a lot of quality goods **to show you**.
  3) **as an adverb** (a verb modifier): I'm working like a horse **to save money**.

A Write down numbers in the blanks as shown below.

> **1,000,000 won**
> **A:** Do you have any TVs for the price under **one million won**?
> **B:** Of course, we do. **There are a lot of quality goods to show you.**

> **2,000,000 won to 2,500,000 won**
> **A:** Do you have any TVs in the price range of **two million won to two million, five hundred thousand won**?
> **B:** I'm sorry. **The goods are currently out of stock.**

1. **3,000,000 won**

   A: Do you have any TVs for the price under
   _____?

   B: Of course, we do. _____

2. **3,000,000 won to 3,500,000 won**

   A: Do you have any TVs in the price range of
   _____?

   B: I'm sorry. _____

3. **4,000,000 won**

   A: Do you have any TVs for the price under _____?
   B: Of course, we do. _____

4. **4,000,000 won to 4,500,000 won**

   A: Do you have any TVs in the price range of
   _____?

   B: I'm sorry. _____

5. **5,000,000 won**

   A: Do you have any TVs for the price under
   _____?

   B: Of course, we do. _____

6. **5,000,000 won to 5,500,000 won**

   A: Do you have any TVs in the price range of
   _____?

   B: I'm sorry. _____

B Fill in the blanks.

3,000,000   A: How much **does it cost to buy** a UHD TV?
　　　　　　　B: It costs at least **three million** won.

2,500,000   A: What **is the price of** the latest model camera?
　　　　　　　B: It is at least **two million, five hundred thousand** won.

1. **1,280,000**

    A: How much _____ a kimchi refrigerator?

    B: It costs at least _____ won.

2. **1,589,990**

    A: What _____ a steam gas dryer?

    B: It is at least _____ won.

3. **1,339,950**

    A: How much _____ an HD camcorder?

    B: It costs at least _____ won.

4. **3,399,000**

    A: What _____ a 4-door French refrigerator with ice dispenser?

    B: It is at least _____ won.

5. **4,187,500**

    A: How much _____ a synthesizer?

    B: It costs at least _____ won.

6. **5,879,000**

    A: What _____ a stereo system?

    B: It is at least _____ won.

7. **8,879,000**

    A: How much _____ a grand piano?

    B: It costs at least _____ won.

3 CONVERSATION

A Work with a partner. Fill in the blanks and practice the conversation.

> **3,000,000**
> A: Wow, how much did you spend on your new **BMW**?
> B: I spent like **thirty million** won on it.
> A: **Thirty million**? I didn't know that you had that much money.
> B: Actually, I've been saving money to buy it.

1 Mercedes / 50,000,000

A: Wow, how much did you spend on your new _____?
B: I spent like _____ won on it.
A: _____? I didn't know that you had that much money.
B: Actually, I've been saving money to buy it.

2 Land Rover / 60,000,000

A: Wow, how much did you spend on your new _____?
B: I spent like _____ won on it.
A: _____? I didn't know that you had that much money.
B: Actually, I've been saving money to buy it.

> ▶ You and your partners are proud housewives bragging about the luxury items that you've recently bought. Try to brag as much as possible. Use the model conversations below.

> A: See? This is my new **Gucci bag**. I paid **10,000,000** won for it!
> B: Oh, yeah? Look at my **Christian Dior shoes**. These are **15,000,000** won a pair!
> A: Really? But did you see my new **Mercedes**? It is **50,000,000** won.

- Chanel bag / 1,370,850
- Burberry coat / 3,276,100
- Prada shoes / 2,956,000
- Louis Vuitton purse / 4,189,500
- Ferragamo boots / 5,234,900
- Hermes bag / 25,000,000

- BMW / 30,000,000
- Land Rover / 60,000,000
- Audi 8 / 80,000,000
- Jeep Cherokee / 70,000,000
- Mercedes / 50,000,000
- Volvo / 90,000,000

B Work with a partner. Fill in the blanks and practice the conversation.

---

your new house / my parents / 1,000,000,000

A: How much **is your new house**?
B: I wouldn't know.
   My parents paid for it.
A: But you can still give me a ball park figure, right?
B: I guess it's about **one billion** won.

---

your new earrings / my husband / 190,000,000

A: How much **are your new earrings**?
B: I wouldn't know.
   My husband paid for them.
A: What is the approximate price?
B: I guess it's about **one hundred and ninety million** won.

---

1. **your dream vehicle / my father / 300,000,000**

   A: How much _____?
   B: I wouldn't know. _____
   A: But you can still give me a ball park figure, right?
   B: I guess it's about _____ won.

2. **your new sofas / my son / 235,600,000**

   A: How much _____?
   B: I wouldn't know. _____
   A: What is the approximate price?
   B: I guess it's about _____ won.

▶ Now you are on your own. Talk about your dream products that you want to buy someday when you are rich enough. Search the internet with your smartphones to look for the approximate price of the items.

A: What's your **dream car**?
B: It's a **Toyota Avalon**.
A: Where does the price range start?
B: It starts from **sixty million** won.
A: How about you?
   What's your dream car?

1. dream car		2. dream house		3. dream bag	
Mercedes	(50,000,000)	house in the southern part of Jeju	(350,000,000)	Chanel	(1,890,000)
Maybach	(500,000,000)	huge residence in Hollywood	(850,000,000)	Prada	(2,990,000)
BMW 6 series	(30,000,000)	house in Hawaii	(450,000,000)	Louis Vuitton	(3,750,000)
Rolls-Royce	(300,000,000)	villa in Malibu beach	(650,000,000)	Burberry	(4,450,000)

C Work with a partner. Fill in the blanks and practice the conversation. 🎧 29

> A: Are you doing anything to make your dreams come true?
> B: **I'm working like a horse** to save money.
> A: What **are you going to do** with the money?
> B: **I'm going to use it to start my own business.**

1. **work all year round / buy a house at the beach**

    A: Is David doing anything to make his dreams come true?
    B: _____ to save money.
    A: What _____ with the money?
    B: _____

2. **work around the clock / build their own house**

    A: Are your parents doing anything to make their dreams come true?
    B: _____ to save money.
    A: What _____ with the money?
    B: _____

▶ Work with a partner. Talk about your saving plans. Ask each other the questions and answer them the expressions in the box.

100,000,000 / found a start-up Internet business

A: What's your goal in saving money?
B: It's **one hundred million** won.
A: What are you doing to achieve the goal?
B: I'm working like a cow day and night.
A: What are you going to do with the money?
B: I'm going to **found a start-up Internet business**.

❶	250,000,000	use it for my parents' retirement
❷	1,000,000,000	buy a building
❸	500,000,000	immigrate to Hawaii and enjoy living there
❹	450,000,000	build a house in Jeju
❺	300,000,000	buy a restaurant and run it
❻	150,000,000	travel all around the world
❼	60,000,000	pay my kids college tuitions
❽	50,000,000	buy my wife a fur coat

Out to the world with Mr. Moon!

READING & WRITING

Read the passage below and answer the questions.

China is a huge country in size. And when it comes to its population, it's even larger. It has approximately 1.4 billion people, which is about 1/4th of the whole human population. When we mention "a megapolis" like Seoul, we usually refer to numbers like ten to twenty million in population. But can you imagine that the Chinese capital city, Beijing, has that of eighty million! When Chinese people talk about "big cities," that means they have at least more than twenty million in population. And when they say, "many people" went home for the holidays, that means that over three hundred million people traveled a long way to visit their hometowns to see the old folks during the lunar New Year's Day season. At least when counting the number of people, the size in China is ten times that of the rest of the world, perhaps.

1. What is the population of China?
→

2. What is the capital of China?
→

3. How large is the population of Beijing?
→

4. At least how many people is a big city supposed to have in China?
→

5. How many people visit their hometowns during the lunar New Year's Day season in China?
→

106 English Fly High | Speeding

WRITING

Tell me about the prices of your household appliances such as TV, refrigerator, washing machine, etc. And how much is your dream car or dream bag? Are you doing anything to make your dreams come true? Write down your answers using the expressions you have learned from this unit.

TV: 1,500,000 (one million, five hundred thousand) won

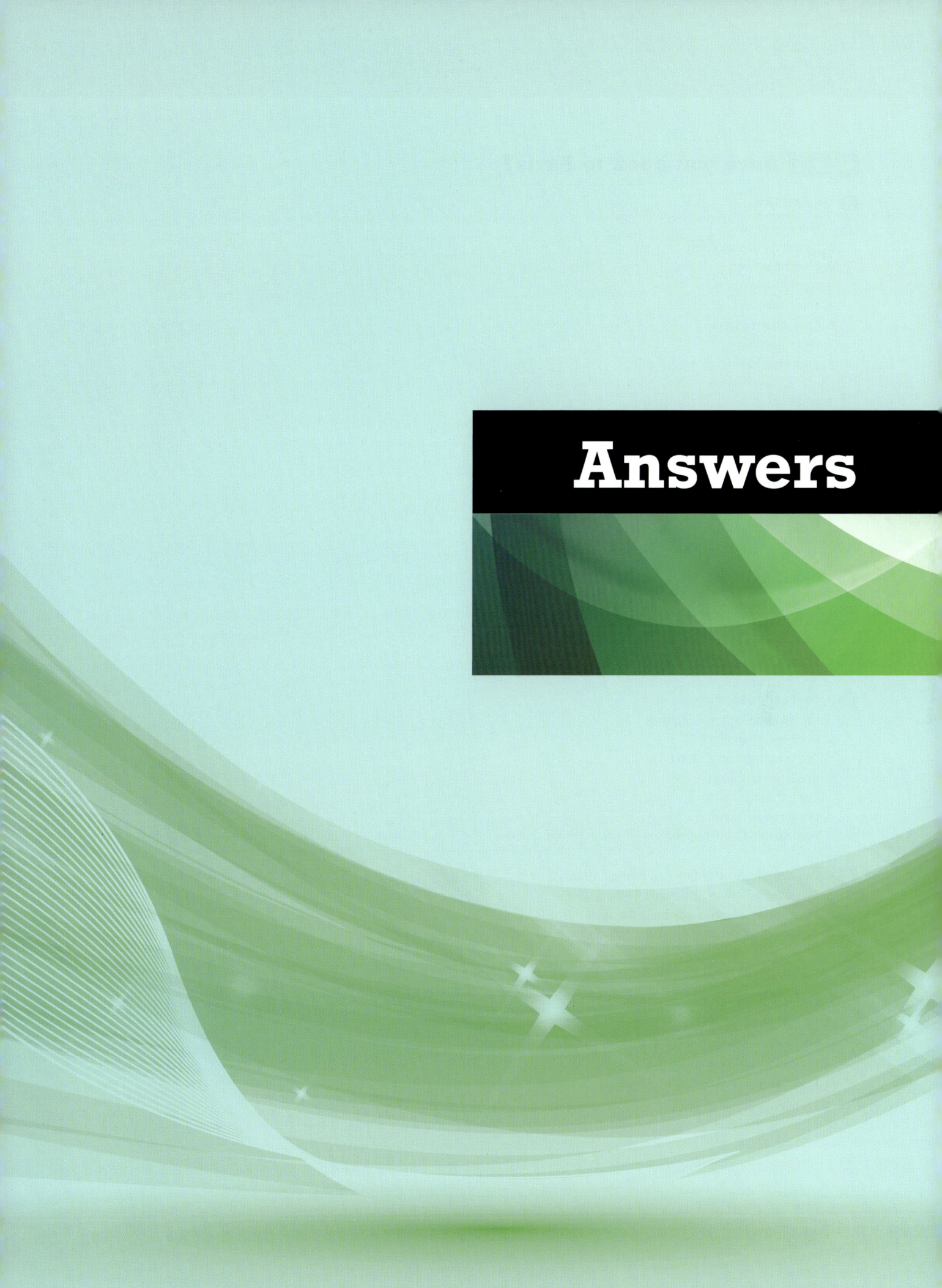

Answers

Unit 1   Have you been to Paris?

❷ GRAMMAR

A
1. saw / have seen
2. traveled / has traveled
3. tried / has tried
4. went / have gone
5. lost / have lost
6. gave / have given
7. met / has met
8. took / has taken

B
1. What
2. How
3. Who(m)
4. How
5. Why
6. How
7. What
8. Who(m)

❸ CONVERSATION

A
1. I have / I've visited Tongyoung.
2. I haven't / I haven't tried *sannakji*.
3. I have / I've visited Paris.
4. I haven't / I haven't tried escargot.

B
1. I've been to Los Angeles.
   I've visited Universal Studios.
2. I've been to Beijing.
   I've seen the Forbidden City.
3. I've been to Busan.
   I've eaten raw fish.
4. I've been to Egypt.
   I've learned belly dancing.

C
1. I've been to Amsterdam / by plane / 10 hours
2. I've visited Denver / by train / 14 hours
3. I've been to Toronto / by bus / 5 hours
4. I've traveled through the Amazon / on foot / 14 days

Out to the world with Mr. Moon
Reading & Writing

1. He has been to three countries.
2. He has been to Vietnam, Cambodia, and the Philippines.
3. It was for business.
4. He visited Europe solely for pleasure.
5. He liked real Italian pasta.

Unit 2 How long have you been doing it?

❷ GRAMMAR

A 1. have been learning
2. has been playing
3. has been driving
4. has been singing
5. have been practicing
6. have been attending
7. have been racing

B 1. since / for
2. since / for
3. since / for
4. for / since
5. since / for
6. since / for
7. for / for

❸ CONVERSATION

A 1. has
been studying Chinese
last year
he has been studying it
3. has
been playing the drums
in high school
she has been playing them

2. have
been learning sign languages
10 years ago
I have been learning them
4. has
been making wine
when he was 20 years old
he has been making it

B 1. cooking Chinese foods
has been cooking Chinese foods
has cooked Japanese foods
3. belly dancing
has been belly dancing
has collected antiques

2. riding a mountain bike
have been riding a mountain bike
have ridden a motor bike

C 1. yachting
it cost too much money
2. knitting
my eyes were sore
3. speed skating
it was too cold

Out to the world with Mr. Moon
Reading & Writing

1. He went scuba diving.
2. No, he wasn't. He got sick of it.
3. He learned chess for three weeks before he won it.
4. Coin collecting made him use up all his savings.
5. That is hobby-seeking itself.

Unit 2 | Answers 111

Unit 3 I should finish the project by today.

❷ GRAMMAR

A
1. must
2. has to
3. ought to
4. need to
5. should
6. ought to
7. have to
8. must

B
1. go on a strike
   we should
   We should go on a strike
3. work out for your health
   I should
   I should work out for my health
5. eat only fruits and vegetables
   you should
   You should eat only fruits and vegetables.
7. apologize in public
   he should
   He should apologize in public.

2. get the credit for graduation
   she doesn't
   She doesn't have to get the credit for graduation.
4. take off our shoes
   we don't
   We don't have to take off our shoes
6. help their son with his homework
   they don't
   They don't have to help their son with his homework.
8. go out
   I don't
   I don't have to go out

❸ CONVERSATION

A
1. he should attend the class
2. she doesn't have to supervise the part-timers
3. they should get a raise
4. you don't have to send a parcel to Betty

B
1. finish this project by 5 o'clock
   do your chemistry homework
2. give my kid some allowance
   give your mom some allowance
3. pay house loans off
   sponsor a charity organization

C
1. work with style
   get fat
2. be very very meticulous
   make typos

Out to the world with Mr. Moon
Reading & Writing

1. It's full of obligations.
2. He thinks his health is not only his but also his family's.
3. He should suffer less income due to a poor outcome at work.
4. He must be a caring and loving father to her.
5. He fulfills them all with a sense of responsibility that comes solely from love.

Unit 4 I am taller than my mother.

❷ GRAMMAR

A
1. thinner
2. richer
3. more beautiful
4. stronger
5. more delicious
6. heavier
7. more expensive

B
1. as smart as
2. not as funny as
3. as old as
4. not as popular as
5. as late as
6. not as crowded as
7. as friendly as

❸ CONVERSATION

A
1. tougher than Mr. Smith but softer than Mr. Sosa
2. slimmer than Jane but chubbier than June
3. colder than yesterday but warmer than last Sunday
4. more expensive than yours but cheaper than Paula's

B
1. smart
   as smart as Mr. Moon
   as smart as Einstein
   as smart as him
2. big
   as big as a calf
   as big as a cow
   as big as a cow
3. handsome
   as handsome as his brother
   as handsome as Tom Cruise
   as handsome as him

C
1. understanding
   your new boss
   much more understanding
2. intriguing
   Christopher Nolan's new movie
   much more intriguing
3. late
   the announcement
   much later

Out to the world with Mr. Moon
Reading & Writing

1. Joseph's father is more meticulous than others.
2. His mother is more understanding than his father.
3. Jane takes after her father in character.
4. No, he isn't taller than her.
5. Joseph's father is as tall as Joseph.

Unit 5   Dogs are the cutest animals.

❷ GRAMMAR

A
1. the wildest
2. the most expensive
3. the laziest
4. the friendliest
5. the tiniest
6. the quietest
7. the most unbelievable

B
1. smiles more brightly than any other gymnast
2. dresses better than any other boy
3. tries harder than any other player
4. calculates more quickly than any other student
5. draws more creatively than any other painter
6. acts more naturally than any other actor
7. sings more perfectly than any other singer
8. dances more beautifully than any other dancer

❸ CONVERSATION

A
1. one of the most expensive
2. one of the rarest
3. one of the fastest
4. one of the biggest

B
1. lizards / stinky / stinkier / snakes / the stinkiest
2. porcupines / tidy / tidier / cats / the tidiest
3. rabbits / gentle / gentler / hamsters / the gentlest

C
1. a lion
   such a scary
   The lion is the scariest
2. a shark
   such a dangerous
   The shark is the most dangerous
3. a prairie dog
   such a funny
   The prairie dog is the funniest

Out to the world with Mr. Moon
Reading & Writing

1. I thought _____ was the toughest animal of all.
2. The cockroach is the toughest animal on the earth.
3. They have existed since the early stages of evolution.
4. Because they can live for years without eating anything.
5. Yes, they can.

Unit 6 What do you plan to do on the weekend?

❷ GRAMMAR

A
1. he is
   He's going to go to the movies.
3. it is
   It's going to arrive.
5. we are
   We're going to go hiking in the mountains.
7. he is
   He's going to leave the office.

2. they are
   They're going to celebrate their wedding anniversary.
4. she will
   She will plant flowers in the garden.
6. she will
   She will work in the family's restaurant.

B
1. does Joe plan to do
   plans to travel the east coast
3. does Tess plan to do
   plans to buy presents for her family at the mall
5. does Angie plan to do
   plans to rest in a pedicure salon
7. do Mr. and Mrs. Williams plan to do
   plan to cook sweet and sour pork together

2. do your children plan to do
   plan to go to ski camp
4. do you and your family plan to do
   plan to visit our ancestors' graves
6. does Mark plan to do
   plans to go to his hometown for a family reunion

❸ CONVERSATION

A
1. Does your son have any plan
   go out with Helen
3. Does Dave have any plan
   work overtime

2. Does your daughter have any plan
   do research at the library

B
1. go to the dentist
   go to the beauty parlor for a perm
2. work over time
   be out of town on business

C
1. this month
   start studying Chinese
   learn some Japanese with me
2. this weekend
   clean the whole house
   go on a blind date with one of my female friends

Out to the world with Mr. Moon
Reading & Writing

1. He has been to the sea for vacation all his life.
2. Because he was severely ill and got an operation on his stomach.
3. He got back on his feet this week.
4. He has hope that he can go to the ocean again.
5. Because he feels like he was born again.

Unit 7 By whom was the speech delivered?

❷ GRAMMAR

A
1. were cared about by the teachers
2. is practiced in gym class by them
3. was solved by Nancy at last
4. is played in the school orchestra by Matthew
5. was made with my classmates by me
6. is eaten in the school cafeteria by students every day
7. is played by Jenny and her friends after school

B
1. will be taken by her next semester
2. is not going to be forgotten by me
3. will be learned with his friends by Charlie
4. is going to be held by us in December
5. is going to be done by Mark this winter vacation
6. won't be eaten by you after dinner
7. is going to be bought by Linda

❸ CONVERSATION

A
1. be elected as a student leader by them this time
   she will be elected as a student leader by them this time
2. used in their class by the students
   they weren't used in their class by the students

B
1. wasn't taken out from the list by Professor Wilson
   was it taken out from the list
   was taken out from the list by Professor Tang
2. wasn't put off by Mandy
   was it put off
   was put off by the principal
3. aren't taken care of by Mrs. Black today
   are they taken care of today
   are taken care of by Mrs. Parker today

C
1. is going to be rung / rang / was rung
2. will be read / read / was read
3. is going to be sung at a school talent show / sang / was sung

Out to the world with Mr. Moon
Reading & Writing

1. It is a Jazz music high school.
2. It was donated by Mr. Anderson, president of the New Orleans Contractors' Society.
3. They were given by the New Orleans Yamaha factory.
4. It was provided by the local Ikea branch.
5. They were given by Apple.
6. The school was built by everyone who has a passionate heart for Jazz music in New Orleans.

Unit 8 Flowers were given to me every day by you.

❷ GRAMMAR

A
1. was bought for his wife by Henry
2. is brought to us by music
3. was written to Ralph by Gina yesterday
4. is always sold to me for half price by her on Thanksgiving Day
5. was made for him by his grandfather last New Year's Day
6. was cooked for us by Ginger
7. were sold to people by the convenience store
8. are still written to my mom by my dad once a week

B
1. is given flowers by Adam every day
   are given to Eve by Adam every day
2. was offered presents and love letters by a lot of fans
   were offered to him by a lot of fans
3. were taught many songs by Mr. Cruise
   were taught to students by Mr. Cruise
4. is going to be found a job by Molly
   is going to be found for Sandra by Molly
5. were asked questions about Halloween costumes by James
   were asked of his friends about Halloween costumes by James
6. were told the story of Santa Claus by Amy
   was told to her children by Amy

❸ CONVERSATION

A
1. was issued to him by the U.S. embassy
   was issued a visa by the U.S. embassy
   he was
2. was told to me by Martha
   were told his secret by Martha
   I was

B
1. he wasn't / was granted to him by the government / he wasn't granted permission by the government
2. she wasn't / was given to her by her colleagues / she wasn't given a surprise farewell party by her colleagues
3. we weren't / was awarded to us by the foundation / you and Don weren't awarded a $10,000 prize by the foundation

C
1. all the people will be interested in
   All the people will be really interested in the big yellow rubber duck.
2. the top of the wedding cake was covered with
   The top of the wedding cake was really covered with white chocolate.
3. Molly is going to be surprised at
   Molly is going to be really surprised at Robin's gift.

Out to the world with Mr. Moon
Reading & Writing

1. He is happiest when he sees his wife happy after she is given presents by him.
2. He always thinks of buying his wife stuff.
3. Because she thinks that too much money is spent on buying her stuff by Sam.
4. "A gift quota" was offered to Sam by Sandy.
5. It's an allotment of money allowed to be spent for the month.
6. 300 dollars are promised to Sam for December by his wife.

Unit 9 What is the price of your new smartphone?

❷ GRAMMAR

 1. twelve thousand won
2. ninety-five thousand won
3. thirty-eight thousand, nine hundred won
4. nineteen thousand, nine hundred won
5. forty-five thousand won
6. fifty-eight thousand, nine hundred (and) thirty won
7. one hundred thousand, fifty won

B 1. more than six hundred thousand
2. less than one hundred thousand
3. more than eight hundred thousand
4. less than three hundred thousand
5. more than four hundred thousand
6. less than two hundred thousand
7. more than nine hundred thousand

❸ CONVERSATION

A 1. this one
   that one
   is it
   It's one hundred (and) thirty-six thousand won.
2. these ones
   those ones
   are they
   They're three hundred (and) twenty thousand won.

B 1. He works as a guard and his job is to keep watch at the bank.
   He gets paid seven hundred thousand
2. They work as dish washers and their job is to wash the dishes at the restaurant.
   They get paid three hundred (and) fifty thousand

C 1. duck down parka looks
   It wasn't
   the duck down parka
   four hundred (and) thirty-six thousand won
   it
2. leather boots look
   they weren't
   the leather boots
   two hundred (and) thirty-eight thousand won
   them

Out to the world with Mr. Moon
Reading & Writing

1. He is a famous actor.
2. They are unexpectedly thrifty.
3. It is forty dollars.
4. It is sixty dollars.
5. He has been donating more than two hundred thousand dollars per year.

Unit 10 How much does it cost to buy a UHD TV?

❷ GRAMMAR

A 1. three million won
   There are a lot of quality goods to show you.
2. three million won to three million, five hundred thousand won
   The goods are currently out of stock.
3. four million won
   There are a lot of quality goods to show you.
4. four million won to four million, five hundred thousand won
   The goods are currently out of stock.
5. five million won
   There are a lot of quality goods to show you.
6. five million won to five million, five hundred thousand won
   The goods are currently out of stock.

B 1. does it cost to buy
   one million, two hundred (and) eighty thousand
2. is the price of
   one million, five hundred (and) eighty-nine thousand, nine hundred (and) ninety
3. does it cost to buy
   one million, three hundred (and) thirty-nine thousand, nine hundred (and) fifty
4. is the price of
   three million, three hundred (and) ninety-nine thousand
5. does it cost to buy
   four million, one hundred (and) eighty-seven thousand, five hundred
6. is the price of
   five million, eight hundred (and) seventy-nine thousand
7. does it cost to buy
   eight million, eight hundred (and) seventy-nine thousand

❸ CONVERSATION

A 1. Mercedes / fifty million / Fifty million
2. Land Rover / sixty million / Sixty million

B 1. is your dream vehicle
   My father paid for it.
   three hundred million
2. are your new sofas
   My son paid for them.
   two hundred (and) thirty-five million, six hundred thousand

C 1. He's working all year round
   is he going to do
   He's going to buy a house at the beach.
2. They're working around the clock
   are they going to do
   They're going to build their own house.

Out to the world with Mr. Moon
Reading & Writing

1. It has approximately 1.4 billion people.
2. It is Beijing.
3. It has the population of eighty million.
4. It's supposed to have at least more than twenty million people.
5. Over three hundred million people visit their hometowns during the season.

Appendix

Grammar Summary

Unit 1

Present Perfect Tense (Have/Has + Past Participle)		
Positives	**Positive Questions**	**WH-Questions**
I have been to Paris.	Have I been to Paris?	Where have I been?
You have been to Paris.	Have you been to Paris?	Where have you been?
He has been to Paris.	Has he been to Paris?	Where has he been?
She has been to Paris.	Has she been to Paris?	Where has she been?
It has been to Paris.	Has it been to Paris?	Where has it been?
We have been to Paris.	Have we been to Paris?	Where have we been?
They have been to Paris.	Have they been to Paris?	Where have they been?
Negatives	**Negative Questions**	
I haven't been to Paris.	Haven't I been to Paris?	
You haven't been to Paris.	Haven't you been to Paris?	
He hasn't been to Paris.	Hasn't he been to Paris?	
She hasn't been to Paris.	Hasn't she been to Paris?	
It hasn't been to Paris.	Hasn't it been to Paris?	
We haven't been to Paris.	Haven't we been to Paris?	
They haven't been to Paris.	Haven't they been to Paris?	

Unit 2

Present Perfect Continuous (Have/Has + Been + Base verb~ing)	
Positives	**Positive Questions**
I have been doing it.	Have I been doing it?
You have been doing it.	Have you been doing it?
He has been doing it.	Has he been doing it?
She has been doing it.	Has she been doing it?
We have been doing it.	Have we been doing it?
They have been doing it.	Have they been doing it?
Negatives	**Negative Questions**
I haven't been doing it.	Haven't I been doing it?
You haven't been doing it.	Haven't you been doing it?
He hasn't been doing it.	Hasn't he been doing it?
She hasn't been doing it.	Hasn't she been doing it?
We haven't been doing it.	Haven't we been doing it?
They haven't been doing it.	Haven't they been doing it?

Unit 3

Modals of Obligation (Should + Base verb)	
Positives	**Questions**
I should do it.	Should I do it?
You should do it.	Should you do it?
He should do it.	Should he do it?
She should do it.	Should she do it?
We should do it.	Should we do it?
They should do it.	Should they do it?
Negatives	**Negative Questions**
I shouldn't do it.	Shouldn't I do it?
You shouldn't do it.	Shouldn't you do it?
He shouldn't do it.	Shouldn't he do it?
She shouldn't do it.	Shouldn't she do it?
We shouldn't do it.	Shouldn't we do it?
They shouldn't do it.	Shouldn't they do it?

- More modals of obligation: must, have to, ought to, be supposed to, be obliged to, need to

Unit 4

Comparatives (Adjective + -er than ~)	
Positives	**Positive Questions**
I'm taller than John.	Am I taller than John?
You're taller than John.	Are you taller than John?
He's taller than John.	Is he taller than John?
She's taller than John.	Is she taller than John?
It's taller than John.	Is it taller than John?
We're taller than John.	Are we taller than John?
They're taller than John.	Are they taller than John?
Negatives	**Negative Questions**
I'm not taller than John.	Aren't I taller than John?
You're not taller than John.	Aren't you taller than John?
He's not taller than John.	Isn't he taller than John?
She's not taller than John.	Isn't she taller than John?
It's not taller than John.	Isn't it taller than John?
We're not taller than John.	Aren't we taller than John?
They're not taller than John.	Aren't they taller than John?

- tall → taller
- easy → easier (y → i)
- big → bigger
- good → better
- beautiful → more beautiful
- bad → worse

Unit 5

Superlatives (Adjective + -est)	
Positives	**Positive Questions**
I'm the tallest.	Am I the tallest?
You're the tallest.	Are you the tallest?
He's the tallest.	Is he the tallest?
She's the tallest.	Is she the tallest?
It's the tallest.	Is it the tallest?
We're the tallest.	Are we the tallest?
They're the tallest.	Are they the tallest?
Negatives	**Negative Questions**
I'm not the tallest.	Aren't I the tallest?
You're not the tallest.	Aren't you the tallest?
He's not the tallest.	Isn't he the tallest?
She's not the tallest.	Isn't she the tallest?
It's not the tallest.	Isn't it the tallest?
We're not the tallest.	Aren't we the tallest?
They're not the tallest.	Aren't they the tallest?

- big → the biggest
- funny → the funniest (y → i)
- beautiful → the most beautiful

Unit 6

Future (Will / Be Going to / Plan to + Base verb)	
Positives	**Positive Questions**
I plan to visit Jim.	Do I plan to visit Jim?
You plan to visit Jim.	Do you plan to visit Jim?
He plans to visit Jim.	Does he plan to visit Jim?
She plans to visit Jim.	Does she plan to visit Jim?
We plan to visit Jim.	Do we plan to visit Jim?
They plan to visit Jim.	Do they plan to visit Jim?
Negatives	**WH-Questions**
I don't plan to visit Jim.	What do I plan to do today?
You don't plan to visit Jim.	What do you plan to do today?
He doesn't plan to visit Jim.	What does he plan to do today?
She doesn't plan to visit Jim.	What does she plan to do today?
We don't plan to visit Jim.	What do we plan to do today?
They don't plan to visit Jim.	What do they plan to do today?

Unit 7

Passive Voice (Be verb + Past Participle)		
Active	Passive	Passive Questions
I saw him.	He was seen by me.	Was he seen by me?
You kissed her.	She was kissed by you.	Was she kissed by you?
He played it.	It was played by him.	Was it played by him?
She hurt me.	I was hurt by her.	Was I hurt by her?
It helped them.	They were helped by it.	Were they helped by it?
They ate kimchi.	Kimchi was eaten by them.	Was kimchi eaten by them?
We killed the bear.	The bear was killed by us.	Was the bear killed by us?
Passive Negatives	WH-Questions	
He wasn't seen by me.	Who was seen by me?	
She wasn't kissed by you.	Who was kissed by you?	
It wasn't played by him.	What was played by him?	
I wasn't hurt by her.	Who was hurt by her?	
They weren't helped by it.	Who were helped by it?	
Kimchi wasn't eaten by them.	What was eaten by them?	
The bear wasn't killed by us.	What was killed by us?	

Unit 8

Passive Voice (Be + P.P. + D.O. / Be + P.P. + to, for, of + I.O.)			
	Active	Passive 1	Passive 2
Positives	I gave her flowers.	She was given flowers by me.	Flowers were given to her by me.
Questions	Did I give her flowers?	Was she given flowers by me?	Were flowers given to her by me?
Negatives	I didn't give her flowers.	She wasn't given flowers by me.	Flowers weren't given to her by me.
Negative Questions	Didn't I give her flowers?	Wasn't she given flowers by me?	Weren't flowers given to her by me?
WH-Questions	Whom did I give flowers to? What did I give her?	Who was given flowers by me?	What were given to her by me?

Unit 9

Numbers under 1,000,000 (a million)				
1,000			**10,000**	
1,000	one thousand		10,000	ten thousand
2,000	two thousand		20,000	twenty thousand
3,000	three thousand		30,000	thirty thousand
4,500	four thousand, five hundred		45,000	forty-five thousand
6,780	six thousand, seven hundred (and) eighty		67,800	sixty-seven thousand, eight hundred
100,000				
100,000	A hundred thousand			
200,000	two hundred thousand			
300,000	three hundred thousand			
450,000	four hundred fifty thousand			
678,000	six hundred (and) seventy-eight thousand			

- **To Infinitive (as a subjective complement)**: My job is **to wait on tables**. (My job = to wait on tables)

Unit 10

Numbers above 1,000,000 (a million)				
1,000,000			**10,000,000**	
1,000,000	one million		10,000,000	ten million
2,000,000	two million		20,000,000	twenty million
3,000,000	three million		30,000,000	thirty million
4,500,000	four million, five hundred thousand		45,000,000	forty-five million
6,780,000	six million, seven hundred (and) eighty thousand		67,800,000	sixty-seven million, eight hundred thousand
100,000,000			**1,000,000,000**	
100,000,000	a hundred million		1,000,000,000	one billion
200,000,000	two hundred million		2,000,000,000	two billion
300,000,000	three hundred million		3,000,000,000	three billion
450,000,000	four hundred (and) fifty million		4,500,000,000	four billion, five hundred million
678,000,000	six hundred (and) seventy eight million		6,780,000,000	six billion, seven hundred (and) eighty million

- **To Infinitive** 1) **as a noun** (subject of a clause): How much does it cost **to buy a UHD TV**?
  2) **as an adjective** (a noun modifier): There are a lot of quality goods **to show you**.
  3) **as an adverb** (a verb modifier): I'm working like a horse **to save money**.